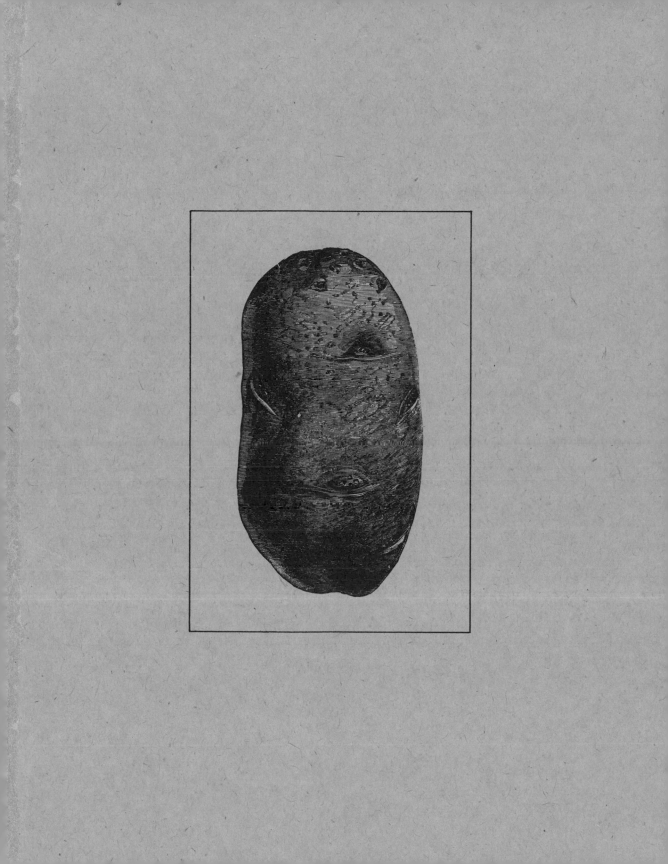

THE
POTATO GARDEN

A Grower's Guide

Maggie Oster

Foreword by Jim Wilson
Illustrations by Lesley Ehlers

Harmony Books
New York

A RUNNING HEADS BOOK

Copyright © 1993 by Quarto Inc.

Published by Harmony Books, 201 East 50th Street,
New York, New York 10022.
Member of the Crown Publishing Group.

HARMONY and colophon are trademarks of
Crown Publishers, Inc.

Library of Congress Cataloging-in-Publication Data

Oster, Maggie.
The potato garden : a grower's guide / Maggie Oster ;
illustrations by Lesley Ehlers.—1st ed.
p.   cm.
Includes bibliographical references (p.   ) and index.
1. Potatoes.   I. Title.
SB211.P8088   1993   92-31649
635'.21—dc20   CIP

THE POTATO GARDEN
A Running Heads Book
Quarto Inc., The Old Brewery,
6 Blundell Street, London N7 9BH

Creative Director: Linda Winters
Senior Editor: Thomas G. Fiffer
Designer: Lesley Ehlers
Production Associate: Belinda Hellinger

Illustrations by Lesley Ehlers

Typeset by Trufont Typographers Inc.

Printed and Bound in Singapore by
Tien Wan Press (Pte) Ltd.

ISBN 0-517-59117-0

1 3 5 7 9 10 8 6 4 2
FIRST EDITION

FOR ILZE,
W.O.S.

ACKNOWLEDGMENTS

Having spent much of my life in search of the perfect order of homefries, as well as mashed potatoes with hot sauce being a staple of my diet, I certainly came to this book with an empathy for the subject. All aspects of food gardening fascinate me, but the thrill of growing something that requires so little care and gives so much reward has always made potatoes high on my list of garden favorites.

For giving me the opportunity of sharing my enthusiasm, I am indebted to John Michel at Harmony Books, whose zeal for the subject was tantamount. Lesley Ehlers kept the hot potato going with her late-night work on the perfect illustrations and delightful design. With aplomb and skill, Tom Fiffer kept the book on track. My thanks to everyone else involved with this book at Harmony and Running Heads, including Marta Hallett, Linda Winters and Josey Ballenger.

Thank you, Jim Wilson, for your foreword to the book and for being a friend and mentor through the years, setting a standard of excellence in communicating your love for gardening and people.

David Ronninger of Ronninger's Seed Potatoes was invaluable and generous in providing information about potato varieties. Thanks also to the National Potato Board and Benny Graves of the Mississippi Sweet Potato Council.

Nothing that I do would be possible without family and friends who give me so much love and support: Jeanne Bargeron, with her humor and ability to face adversity with savoir faire; Art and Chris Cestaro, who fed me pasta when I could no longer think about potatoes; Allen and Lorie Farmer, who filled the farm with happiness again; John Grammer, with his music and words, ever there, ever enough; Lynne Gream, who taught me the finer points of golf and friendship; Kurt Hampe, for the computer help, cheering phone calls, and flowers; Kimberly Hillerich, whose great sweet potato cake recipe didn't get used; Heather Middleton, for sharing those moments of vented anger and laughter; Arlo Minden, for long-distance longevity; Justin Reiter, who is steadfastly amazing; Susan Roth, graciously providing empathy as a writer and friend; William Scott, for great ideas and timely help from England; Sueann Townsend, who reminds me that pain is my friend and passion for work is good; Peter Watson, for the art and the encouragement to be preposterous; Chris Woods, with his definitive volumes on potato taxonomy and skewed perspective; and my parents, with their enthusiasm for gardening and food.

I can never begin to thank Ilze Meijers enough, both for her indefatigable research and for being the best cosmic twin anyone could ever hope to have.

CONTENTS

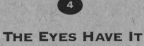

TUBER LOVING CARE

ONE POTATO TWO POTATO

THIS SPUD'S FOR YOU

DO THE MASHED POTATO

FOREWORD

Potatoes helped to save my life. They really did. It was during the Great Depression, when I was not yet a teenager. My father, laid off and penniless, grew market crops to sell for cash and to help keep our large family fed.

Those were precarious times, from 1929 until the late 1930s. Families in our part of Mississippi existed from one crop to the next, because there was little or no money to buy soap and food staples, much less amenities such as coffee, tea and salt. Our preferred carbohydrates were cornmeal and rice, but the weevils often ruined corn in the crib within a few months, and rice cost money. Thus potatoes were very important to us, both Irish and sweet. Seed potatoes were relatively cheap, and Mr. Broome of Vicksburg Seed and Feed kindly extended us credit until some of the harvest could be sold. We grew our own sweet potato slips in large concrete hotbeds, filled with dry brush and firewood, which was burned to sterilize the soil and to supply nutrient-rich ashes.

With such a background, it is difficult for me to appreciate the humor in potatoes. Only in recent years have I been able to loosen up and enjoy potato jokes, poetry and songs. Vincent van Gogh had the same problem; witness his grim painting, *The Potato Eaters*. I outgrew my potato hangups; he sacrificed an ear to his.

We had our own bittersweet potato songs in the South. I can remember "Take a Cold Tater and Wait," Nashville's version of a mother's response to a hungry child, impatient for suppertime to come. The song referred to sweet potatoes of course: Cold Irish potatoes taste good only in potato salad or that cold potato soup with the fancy French name.

My friend Maggie Oster relates many a way to plant Irish potatoes, which for lack of a better name she refers to as "common" potatoes. But she couldn't know how we planted them in our peculiar, yellow, wind-deposited loessial soil. My father hitched a middle-buster plow behind a strong mule and swept wide, shallow furrows on a contour around a hill. He scattered chicken manure over the furrows and pitched in a six-inch (15-cm) layer of spoiled hay left over from the Johnson grass harvest, hand scythed and stacked around a locust log upright. Then he laid seed potato pieces, cut the day before and allowed to dry, one foot (30.5 cm) apart atop the half-decomposed hay. He then dressed on another six-inch (15-cm) layer of hay and threw a layer of soil atop it to keep the hay from blowing away. As I recall, it was just before my birthday when we planted Irish potatoes, which would have made it early February.

Maggie, a dedicated organic gardener, would have fainted dead away had she seen how we controlled Colorado potato beetles. We filled small cloth bags with Paris Green (would you believe lead arsenate?), held them above the foliage and tapped them with a stick until the foliage was whitish green with dust. It killed the beetles and larvae, and would have killed us had we done it more often than once or twice a season. Maybe that is why my old bones ache so now: arsenic is an accumulative poison that never fully disappears.

Around the time we saw the first metallic green June bugs, we "grappled" for new potatoes. It was very gratifying, groping around in the warm, compacted layer of near-humus for tubers. I don't remember the name of the red variety we planted, but it made loads of mighty fine potatoes. We harvested only as many at a time as we could sell or eat. They were all gone before the soil grew so hot that they would spoil. I believe the layer of rotting organic matter helped to insulate the tubers from the fast-heating soil.

Irish potatoes were crucial to our early summer diet because they came on just as the mustard greens had shot to seed and before roasting ears were ready from the 'Mexican June' corn growing in the bottomland. Nature arranged for 'Kentucky Wonder' string beans (lord, did they have strings in those days) to mature just in time to boil with the new potatoes. We never got fancy with cooking new potatoes. No parsley, no herbs, just boiled or fried potatoes or rarely (because cheese was expensive) potatoes au gratin.

We transplanted the sweet potato slips to ridged-up rows just after the pecan trees leafed out. Oh, they would look sorry, even after we toted water down the rows and baptized each transplant with a dipper full. Between then and harvest the spreading vines didn't ask much from us, except that we pull the occasional overtopping pigweed or watergrass. If the sweet potatoes got off to a quick start, we would often take tip cuttings and set them into adjacent rows. If we watered them in, the cuttings would usually "take" regardless of their lack of roots.

In mid-November, after a light frost or two, we would plow out the dark-skinned, intensely sweet 'Porto Rican' (no one called them "Puerto Rican") potatoes and cure them in a hot room that quickly reduced their moisture content. After a couple of weeks of curing we would hide the roots in the hayloft under layers of our choice cutting of hay, kept for feeding the horses and mules. An enormous black rat snake kept the barn varmints under control; we knew to leave him be because he protected our winter food supply.

To this day I dearly love sweet potatoes. I long for the soft sweetness of the true 'Porto Rican' variety but can't buy them anywhere. That was the variety that the canny Louisiana commercial growers so successfully marketed as "yams" early in this century. Now it has been replaced by more productive, better keeping, more disease-resistant varieties that are, to my connoisseur's palate, good but certainly not great. All of them, 'Nancy Hall', 'Centennial', 'Georgia Red', are rather dry and mealy, and only passably sweet. Today's 'Porto Rican' isn't the same as we grew; of that I am sure.

If you think I am overstating the case by remembering potatoes as saving my life, picture this: Father is down in the bottoms all day long, behind a mule-drawn cultivator. Mother is in the hospital having another baby. Grandma is keeping the younger children. I am home alone, just me and the baked sweet potatoes. After all, someone has to feed the chickens and look after the calves and shoats. Grandma had cooked sweet potatoes for us the previous night, and along with them, a pan of biscuits from scratch. She left them in the warming oven atop the wood range. Along about noontime, Father comes up from the fields, hungry for what we called "dinner." Out from the icebox comes a pound of home-churned butter, a piece of fried sidemeat from a day or two ago, and a crock of sweet milk. Split the sweet potato, wedge in a chunk of butter, sozzle a biscuit in the milk . . . heavenly!

Mother and Grandma cooked sweet potatoes in every way known to mankind, I am sure. Baked and served in the skins; sliced and fried; baked, mashed and filled into piecrusts or casserole dishes . . . perhaps for Christmas the sweet potato pies would be topped with marshmallows. Funerals in the South, always an occasion for taking food to the bereaved, brought out the best sweet potato pies under the sun.

My knuckles hurt when I think about harvesting sweet potatoes. The last year we lived on the farm, just before Father got a job in Memphis, we harvested a bumper crop of sweet potatoes. Autumn came early and brought unusually cold weather. We had to hurry to get the potatoes out of the field and cured before they spoiled from the cold. I was fourteen and was expected, not unreasonably, to do a man's work. No one had gloves, not even warm coats. Teeth chattering, hands cracked and blue, we tried to balance the careful handling required by sweet potatoes with the need to hurry. We saved the crop, and the profits from selling it helped to buy us the first restaurant meal I can remember, in the then-grand Illinois Central Railroad depot in Memphis.

You can understand, then, why I read *The Potato Garden* with uncommon interest . . . you might even say with visceral involvement. Maggie grew up on a farm as I did, but in a much later era when there was more to laugh and kid about. She has travelled a great deal, and it shows in her how-to-grow and harvest instructions; they are applicable all over the country. I agree with all of her information with but one small caveat. She believes in companion crops; I don't, not now at least.

I'm sure that Maggie never realized when she was researching the history of potatoes that she would clear up a mystery that has puzzled me all my life, the derivation of the term *croker sack*. I took for granted that burlap bags were called croker sacks, because we used them to hold the frogs or "croakers" from a night of bullfrog-gigging. Now she tells me that "croker" was an old Irish name for potatoes! It figures; I lived in a heavily Scotch-Irish neighborhood.

Now that I can afford all the rice, cornmeal and wheat flour that I could possibly want, I find myself turning away from them to potatoes, both common and sweet. My microwave has made the difference. I can prepare potatoes in a jiffy. But now, instead of a wedge of butter, it's a gob of low-fat cottage cheese on my Irish potatoes and the teeniest smidgen of margarine on my sweet potatoes. The potatoes I buy from the store are good, but not as good as home-grown, and they certainly can't compare with gourmet varieties. I intend to use Maggie's book in locating gourmet potatoes and sources this coming spring, without fail. Growing potatoes today is so easy that it makes me feel like a dilettante gardener, but I can learn to live with that!

—Jim Wilson

ONE

Reigning Potatoes

HISTORY OF THE POTATO

The road to hell may be paved with good intentions, but the path of man's history and culture seems influenced more by the vagaries of chance. The far-reaching ramifications of any act are seldom apparent, even to the wisest and most prescient people. Hairpin twists and turns in the evolution of a nation or a people may hinge on the most untoward or seemingly innocuous of words, actions, or objects. Only time gives us any perspective.

Witness the potato.

What Spanish soldier-storyteller of the 1500s could have begun to concoct a tale of how some insignificant small, knobby roots grown by the Incas in the Andean high sierra would someday become the most popular vegetable in the world?

How barren our tables— and how different our lives— would be without tomatoes, beans, corn, squash, peppers, chocolate, and potatoes, and the roles each have played in world politics. Beans may have a slight edge nutritionally, but no food has been so widely adapted around the globe as the potato: it has found a place as a staple in the diets of nearly every people. Although unrelated, if both sweet and common potatoes are considered together, they can be grown in a range of soils and growing conditions from sea level to altitudes of fifteen thousand feet (4,572 m)—a much wider range than virtually any other crop.

So why not grow a little piece of destiny in your own backyard this year? Potatoes are productive plants for the home garden *plus* a nutritious and versatile addition to the dinner table. They are among the most efficient vegetables you can grow in terms of food value for space, yielding twenty-five pounds (11 kg) from a twenty-five foot (7.5 m) row and containing significant amounts of protein, minerals and vitamins. Using easy, centuries-old techniques, you will be surprised at what you can grow with a minimal amount of labor in a small amount of space.

Another reason to grow your own potatoes is to sample some of the over two hundred varieties available commercially, and their remarkable range of flavors, textures and colors. Most important, your home-grown potatoes can truly be a comfort food when you know they've been raised without damaging chemicals.

How much do you really know about potatoes? There are many misconceptions and erroneous assumptions. Mythic though the potato may be, *The Potato Garden* is an attempt to sort out fact and fiction, both to entertain readers and to encourage more people to grow this remarkably versatile food.

THE RECORD HOLDER IN THE *GUINNESS BOOK OF WORLD RECORDS* FOR POTATO CRISP (CHIP) CONSUMPTION IS WILLIE NEWGENT OF ARMAGH, ENGLAND, WHO ATE THIRTY BAGS WITHOUT A DRINK IN 24 MINUTES, 33.6 SECONDS.

All studies indicate that both common and sweet potatoes probably originated in South America. Carbon dating of ancient peels of wild common potato tubers discovered in Chile has shown them to be at least eleven thousand years old. The oldest *cultivated* potato is thought to be ten thousand years old. Grains from the fertile crescent were cultivated no earlier than potatoes were in the New World.

The Andes mountain range influences the climate of vast

WESTERN
HEMISPHERE

parts of South America. Although much of the continent lies in the tropic zones, the high altitudes and the humidity changes created by the steep mountains make for a variety of weather, much of it harsh. The common potato was first discovered and eaten, then cultivated, in these upper, cooler regions of Colombia, Ecuador, Peru, Bolivia and Chile, with most found at altitudes between fifteen hundred (457 m) and twelve thousand five hundred feet (3,810 m). Maize, or corn, was grown in other regions of South America, but it would not grow above eleven thousand feet (3,352 m). Historians believe the discovery of the potato actually enabled South American people to inhabit the highlands.

Some two hundred species of wild common potatoes still exist in an area stretching from the southwestern United States to Chile. Most have small, bitter tubers. The potatoes we enjoy today are the result of centuries of selection and both unintentional and intentional cross-breeding . . . mostly from a handful of species. Only in the past century or so have plant breeders gone back to the wild in an effort to diversify the gene pool and

> IN EARLY IRISH POTATO GROWING, SEED POTATOES WERE PLANTED ON GOOD FRIDAY.

improve the growth and nutritional value of potatoes.

For the natives of Central and South America, the potato proved a versatile, reliable source of food, especially given their method of preserving it in a somewhat freeze-dried form known as *chuno*. Adopted by the Incan culture as it developed and spread its influence over the indigenous tribes stretching twenty-five hundred miles (4,023 km) from Ecuador through Peru, Chile, and Argentina, *chuno* provided excellent portable rations for the Incan armies. The pottery of the Incas and other natives alludes often to the potato, confirming its importance in their culture. Potatoes have been discovered in tombs, are thought to have played a part in religious rites, and were used to decorate pots and even whistles. Further evidence of the potato's preeminence is reflected in today's descendants of the Incas, the Quechua Indians, who have over a thousand different words for potato.

The first European to encounter sweet potatoes was Christopher Columbus, on his second voyage to the New World. Along with assorted natives, parrots, and gold, he sent the sweet potato back to Spain in 1494. Sweet potatoes quickly assumed the role of a luxury delicacy in Spain and were taken to other shores. They were a particular favorite of England's Henry VIII, especially when baked into pies. By Shakespeare's time the sweet potato was considered an aphrodisiac, with dried, sugared slices sold by street vendors. In 1599 Shakespeare wrote *The Merry Wives of Windsor*, in which Falstaff's cry, "Let the sky rain potatoes," refers to the sweet potato. Over the years, the sweet potato continued to go in and out of fashion as a love potion, even in the court of Napoleon's Jos-

ephine. Japanese homeopaths still prescribe them to improve fertility.

The common potato, which may be white, yellow, pink, red, blue, purple or black, did not meet with such immediate success. Francisco Pizarro's exploits in Ecuador and Peru—conquering the Incas between 1531 and 1533 and plundering their wealth—brought him into contact with the Incas' starchy staple, which he or perhaps another conquistador, described as a "tasty, mealy truffle," and included in cargo sent back to Spain. Spanish conquerors in Chile were also aware of potatoes, but they did not acquire a

taste for them as readily as those in Peru, and it was the Peruvian name for the food, *papas*, which the Spanish adopted. Comparing potatoes to boiled chestnuts and referring to them as "earth nuts," the Spanish conquerors ate them in various ways, and even made flour from potatoes for baking breads, cakes, and other delicacies.

Although the exact date of

> **THE POTATOES NEVER FAILED US. . . . FOR EACH MEAL, THEY LOOKED DIFFERENT AND TASTED DIFFERENT.**
>
> *One Foot in America*
> Yuri Suhl

> **POTATO: BLAND, AMIABLE, AND HOMELY, AN HONEST VEGETABLE, GIVING HONOUR WHERE HONOUR IS DUE—IN AN HONEST SOUP."**
>
> Della Lutes
> *The Country Kitchen*, 1938

introduction to Spain is impossible to verify, Cieza de Leon mentioned the potato in his *Cronica de Peru*, published in Seville in 1553. A study of the plants in Spain in 1564, however, did not mention the potato. Still, there are written records of potatoes being eaten in a hospital in Seville in 1573.

The meanderings of the potato across the European continent were measured, to say the least. Common potatoes were first introduced into Italy in 1585, but didn't arrive in Sweden until 1765, when a government edict forced the peasants to grow them. Now, of course, potatoes are a major food in all of Scandinavia, more so than in Italy. Peter the Great took potatoes home to Russia after a visit to Holland in 1697.

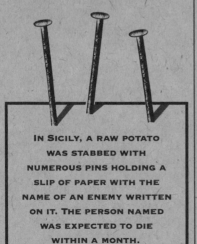

IN SICILY, A RAW POTATO WAS STABBED WITH NUMEROUS PINS HOLDING A SLIP OF PAPER WITH THE NAME OF AN ENEMY WRITTEN ON IT. THE PERSON NAMED WAS EXPECTED TO DIE WITHIN A MONTH.

The English began growing potatoes as early as 1586. The first description of the common potato in an English scientific publication was written in 1596 by John Gerard, an amateur English botanist compiling a catalogue of plants. Gerard received roots from Virginia (possibly from Sir Francis Drake), which he referred to as "common potato," *Batatta virginiana*, Virginian potatoes, and *Pappus*, creating confusion with the name for the sweet potato as well as the country of origin. The West Indian name for sweet potato, *batata*, played a role in the etymology of the word *potato*, with much confusion existing among sweet potatoes, yams, and the common potato until at least the late 1700s. Many other writers would add to the misinformation about this new plant over the ensuing centuries. Gerard did accurately describe them as tasty when roasted in the fire or boiled

and eaten with oil, vinegar, and pepper.

Gerard's misrepresentation was probably the result of what might be labelled the great Virginia mix-up. It seems that Sir Francis Drake, on the way home from pirating Spanish vessels in the Caribbean, stopped for supplies—including potatoes—in Cartagena, Colombia. The story goes that during a stopover at Roanoke, Drake gave some of the tubers to Sir Walter Raleigh's agent, hence they reached Raleigh's Irish estate near Cork. An addendum is that either Drake or Raleigh supposedly gave some to Queen Elizabeth I, whose cooks fed the court the toxic stems and leaves rather than the knobby roots, setting back common potato consumption in England by some years.

Gerard continued to expound on potatoes in subsequent editions of his herbal, giving "Spanish" potatoes a chapter of their own. Another herbalist, John Parkinson, recognized three "potatoes": the Virginia, the Spanish and the Jerusalem artichoke. From the latter part of the 1500s through much of the 1700s the common potato was regarded with a mixture of fascination and skepticism throughout Europe and England.

Initially, the common potato was a botanical curiosity, with its attributes discussed endlessly. Because the tomato and Jerusalem artichoke arrived in Europe at about the same time as the potato, the three plants were often confused, with much superstition attached to all. Due to the potato's relationship to the poisonous nightshades and the toxicity of its foliage and fruit, the potato was frequently feared. Even those who promoted it did not like the purple skin and yellow flesh of the early South American tubers, and Europeans immediately set out to grow pale, more uniform tubers.

THE TRADITIONAL IRISH DISH CALLED COLCANNON IS MASHED POTATOES MIXED WITH COOKED ONIONS AND KALE OR CABBAGE. ALWAYS EATEN AT HALLOWEEN, COLCANNON TELLS ONE'S FORTUNE. TRINKETS STIRRED INTO THE MIXTURE AND THEIR MESSAGES INCLUDE A BUTTON FOR A BACHELOR, A THIMBLE FOR AN OLD MAID, A RING FOR A MARRIAGE WITHIN THE YEAR, A COIN FOR WEALTH AND A HORSESHOE FOR GOOD FORTUNE.

Because the potato was a food plant grown from a tuber rather than a seed, symbolism was sometimes drawn from the humanoid shapes of deformed tubers. Also, over time, potatoes accrued a considerable list of alleged medicinal benefits, including curing sore backs, rheumatism, sore throats, sunburn, frostbite, ill temper, warts, cholera, toothache, black eyes and drunkenness. The method of growing the potato, without using the seed, was considered incestuous and, therefore, evil. That the potato was not mentioned in the Bible was further cause to regard it with suspicion, especially in the case of the conservative elements of the Orthodox Russian Church and the Scots Presbyterians. In the 1700s, potatoes became known as "the Devil's apples." Sugar and tobacco were also included in this list of abominations.

The French refused at first to eat the new food, claiming it caused sexual misconduct, leprosy, syphilis, scrofula and flatulence. The soil was said to be destroyed where it was planted. Finally they declared it edible, although the upper classes decided it "tasted insipid and starchy." Even in the late 1700s the potato was still not widely eaten in France. Naturalist Raoul Combes described it in 1749 as the "worst of all vegetables."

Antoine-Augustin Parmentier, an agricultural chemist, promoted the potato in France after he survived the Seven Years' War as a German prisoner of war eating not much else but potatoes. He studied potato cultivation and nutrition and won a prize in 1771 for their virtues in a treatise. Many Frenchmen joked that he invented potatoes and tried to force them on his countrymen. One problem with Parmentier's presentation was his emphasis on the potato as a source of flour, the best use of which at the time proved to be whitening wigs. Only when he won over Louis XVI and Marie Antoinette did the potato become trendy. Among his accomplishments was the supervision of a court feast with more than twenty potato

dishes. For posterity, Parmentier is immortalized in the French potato soup, *potage parmentier.*

Germans took to potatoes with a bit more *schnell.* By 1581 the first known potato recipes were printed, by no less than Johannes Gutenberg. In the early 1700s, Prussian Emperor Frederick William I issued an edict ordering all peasants to plant potatoes or else have their noses and ears cut off! His grandson, Frederick the Great, used a gentler approach, choosing to eat potatoes himself and to provide seed potatoes to landowners. His reign is noted for, among other skirmishes, the War of Bavarian Succession in 1778–79, more commonly known as the Kartoffelkrieg, or Potato War, because potato fields were the site of much of the fighting.

Over time, country by country, the potato was recognized as a highly productive plant, providing at least five times as much food per acre than grains such as wheat or rye. Though competing at first with the Jerusalem artichoke, the potato proved more easily digestible with a milder and more versatile flavor. As a filling and nutritious source of carbohydrates, the potato was unbeatable.

In 1683, the Royal Society of London promoted potatoes as being well suited for feeding the poor, and in many countries, the upper classes

THE INEBRIATED POTATO

Nearly every country where potatoes have been widely grown has managed to make some sort of alcoholic beverage from them. Or, as poet Chet Vittitow pointed out, vodka begins with mashed potatoes. Vodka itself actually was first made from wheat or rye in the 1300s by the Russians, but potatoes proved infinitely more efficacious. The Russians have also used potatoes to make schnapps. The Incas made a brew from the tubers called *chakta*, while a present-day Peruvian beer is called *chicha*. Of course, the Irish had plenty of raw material to create the high-octane *poteen*, which is now illegal to make in Ireland. Some of the Scandinavian *aquavit*, the water of life and the traditional beverage for toasting at smorgasbords, is distilled from fermented potato mash, then flavored with caraway, citrus, cardamom, anise and fennel. Eighteenth-century Americans turned potatoes into whiskey and wine. To the Alaskan gold miners of the 1890s we can gratefully acknowledge the slang "hooch," a condensation of the *Hoochinoo* tribe, for their potato-distilled beverage.

presented potatoes as a splendid answer to the gnawing problem of feeding the peasants. The masses of many countries were encouraged, if not pressured, to use the potato as a staple food. And that is what it became worldwide. Some historians believe the potato helped fuel the industrial revolution. Free of many of the epidemic diseases associated with grains, populations grew in numbers. The surplus people who were not needed on the farms went to cities to find work, creating a supply of labor, which could, of course, be fed cheaply with potatoes. Political power shifted in the Western world, as northern countries, where the potato had become a staple food, became more powerful than those in southern Europe.

The history of the potato, both in its native land and all over the globe, is two-sided. As a productive, easily grown, adaptable, year-round source of excellent nutrition, the potato has nurtured and sustained many millions of people. But, as Redcliffe Salaman writes in *The History and Social Influence of the Potato*, the potato is "a weapon ready forged for the exploitation of a weaker group in a mixed society." Witness its use in Ireland.

Before 1650, the potato was primarily a garden crop used mostly as a cattle food in Europe, but in Ireland it had already become a staple food crop for humans. How and when the potato actually arrived in Ireland is not clear. Perhaps a member of the Spanish Armada left a few behind, although some people give credit to Sir Walter Raleigh. Regardless of who brought potatoes to Ireland, by 1606 they were an accepted crop, and by 1620, a crucial one. Only fifty years after its introduction, it had become the primary food in most of Ireland, long before it was generally accepted in the rest of the British Isles. It took over one hundred fifty years for the potato to become part of the English general diet, where it never became the primary source of nutrition.

Ireland's geographical position as an isolated island with limited trade, few natural resources and little wealth, as well as its small population, agricultural economy (based on cattle as wealth), and entrenched local customs, contributed to the potato's immense popularity and influence. Also, Ireland's cool, windy, damp climate was well suited to potatoes and poor for growing grains. A lack of iron, copper or tin ore limited indigenous farming tools to the more primitive, less efficient wooden implements, which also made grain production difficult.

> "POTATOES, LIKE WIVES, SHOULD NEVER BE TAKEN FOR GRANTED."
>
> Peter Pirbright
> *Off The Beaten Track*, 1946

Ireland's political and social climate was also unique. The personal relationship of man to soil was absent, with a long history of communal cultivation. The English tenancy system established in Ireland by the sixteenth century required farmers to work absentee landlords' fields in return for enough money to pay the rent and feed themselves on what little land was left. Cromwell's method of enforcing English domination of Ireland was to starve the natives out. The potato was their last resort and allowed the survival of the half of the Irish population Cromwell failed to wipe out. No other single food could feed a family and its livestock as well as the potato.

A five hundred- to eight hundred-yard (457 to 733 m) deep-mulched bed of potatoes could feed a family, with a supplement of milk, pork, cheese and cow's blood. If potatoes were the *only* food, a longer bed could be planted. A small plot of land could support a family of six, pro-

viding hundreds of pounds of tubers each week, rounded out with relatively tiny amounts of oatmeal, milk and salted fish.

Between 1760 and 1840, the Irish population rose from 1.5 million to 9 million, an increase of 600 percent. On the existing land, if bread had been the staple, only 5 million could have been fed. The Irish soon began to depend almost solely on the potato for subsistence, on the farm and in the cities. A factory worker's daily allotment was twelve pounds (5.5 kg).

Then a worldwide shortage of affordable grain in the late 1700s doubled its price, and potato diseases started to find the tubers. In 1750, dry rot

"MANY BATTLES WERE FOUGHT. BUT SOMETIMES AFTER A BATTLE THE GENERAL LOOKED AT HIS MUDDIED UNIFORM AND BENT SWORD, AND THOUGHT OF A BAKED POTATO AND A SOFT BED."

Anita Löbel
Potatoes, Potatoes, 1967

appeared, then curl was reported in 1770. *Botrytis cinerea*, a mold, first showed up in Ireland in 1795. Blackleg appeared in 1833 and late blight, *Phytophthora infestans*, on the Isle of Wight in 1845. The earlier diseases caused some small-scale potato failures, with several classed as famines, but these were interspersed with good years and mostly localized.

Blight, however, hit hard and fast. The first winter of the Great Potato Famine was 1845–46. The lack of modern communication methods delayed widespread knowledge of the scope of the crisis, but through the newspapers that did exist, word slowly began to disseminate. By the time public sympathy was aroused, it was too late to prevent disaster. The number of dead was staggering—over 1 million according to most

estimates—with a figure of 2.5 million not unrealistic. Another estimated 1.5 million emigrated.

Although Drake may have left some tubers behind at the Roanoke Colony, the "official" arrival of the potato in Colonial America was in 1622, as a present from the governor of Bermuda to the governor of Virginia. Lion Gardiner, a settler of Saybrook, Connecticut, wrote in 1636 to John Winthrop Jr., requesting some potatoes to plant as he had been taught by some "Virginians." Most likely his wishes were granted, as early

records include the delivery of fifteen tons (14 MT) to the Massachusetts Bay Colony in 1636. Potatoes also appeared on a dinner menu celebrating a new president of Harvard in 1707. The best-known early effort at growing potatoes was in 1719 by a settlement of Scotch-Irish in what was then Londonderry, now Derry, New Hampshire. By 1720 in Connecticut and 1735 in Rhode Island, potatoes were being raised as a food crop.

George Washington planted potatoes at his Mount Vernon plantation in 1767. In

Thomas Jefferson's gardening notes from Monticello, he lists Indian, Irish, long, round, seed and sweet potatoes. In what is basically considered the first American gardening book, the mid-1700s *Treatise on Gardening*, John Randolph Jr. leans heavily on English information, suggesting that potatoes be planted either in a light sandy loam or by the Irish method of deep mulching.

Potatoes did not come into their own in the United States until the 1800s, with the wave of immigrants who relied so heavily on potatoes,

most notably the Irish, as well as Germans, Poles and others. The Gaelic influence was so great that for many people the common potato was, and still is, referred to as the Irish potato.

In America's first published cookbook, *American Cookery*, published in 1796, Amelia Simmons mentions five varieties of potatoes. From other sources of this era, another dozen or so names crop up. With the decimation worldwide of potato crops from the blight (which also reduced the American crop by 40 percent), interest was piqued to find blight-

THE FAVORITE FOOD OF PAUL CEZANNE WAS POTATOES WITH OLIVE OIL.

resistant varieties. The Commonwealth of Massachusetts offered a $10,000 prize to whomever found "a sure and practical remedy for the Potato Rot." The result was that by the mid-1800s there were at least a hundred varieties and more being added each year.

A major contributor to the nineteenth-century effort of developing new strains of potatoes, in effect if not directly in number of varieties, was the pioneer American plant breeder Luther Burbank. From his farm in Lunenburg, Massachusetts, the young man in his early twenties began a selection process. Eventually, he chose one and sold it to nurseryman J. J. H. Gregory for $150, a sum he used to move to California. That potato, which came to be known as the Burbank, was the forerunner of the ubiquitous "baking," "Idaho," or Russet-type potato. Approximately a billion dollars' worth of this type of potato has been grown commercially in the past fifty years.

Today, potato varieties number in the thousands, but

HANDWARMER

VICTORIAN LADIES IN ENGLAND WORE MUFFS TO KEEP THEIR HANDS WARM IN THE WINTER. TO MAKE THE MUFF EVEN MORE COZY, STREET VENDORS SOLD HOT POTATOES TO GO INSIDE. A CERAMIC VERSION, MEANT TO BE FILLED WITH HOT WATER, WAS ALSO MADE.

VITAMIN C

about 80 percent of the American crop derives from a few cultivars, with nearly half the commercial common potato crop being Russet type and 75 percent of the sweet potato crop being 'Jewell'. Common potato production in the world today almost tips the scale at 300 million tons (273 million MT) annually, making potatoes the largest crop behind sugar cane, wheat, rice, maize, and sugar beets. Ranking ninth is the sweet potato with 100 million tons (91 million MT) produced each year. Until the Soviet Union's recent disbanding, it was the top potato-growing country, producing about 25 percent of the world's crop, much of it going to feed livestock or distilled into vodka. The Chinese, with the second largest crop, feed a lot of potatoes to pigs but are learning

to make potato chips. Following in line are Poland, Germany, the United States and Ireland.

About 14.5 million tons (13.2 million MT) of potatoes are produced in the United States each year, with Idaho accounting for 8.5 million (7.7 million MT) of that. Other major potato-producing states include Washington, Maine, Oregon, Colorado and Wisconsin.

Although the sweet potato preceded the common potato to Europe and was more immediately accepted, its preference for a warm climate precluded acceptance at the level of the common potato. Nevertheless, it has become an important crop in warmer regions all over the world. Sweet potatoes reached their heyday in the United States in the first half of the twentieth century. Noted American botanist, agricultural chemist and educator George Washington Carver devised over a hundred uses for the crop and issued over four dozen bulletins on the subject between 1898 and 1943, convincing many southern farmers to grow sweet potatoes instead of cotton. Carver's goal was as much to improve nutrition as farmers' finances.

The average annual American consumption of sweet potatoes has declined from a high of about twenty pounds (9 kg) in the 1940s to about five pounds (2.5 kg) per year now. Interest in this crop, which tolerates poor soil, droughts, and many pests and has high levels of vitamins and minerals is now in a revival. Louisiana, Mississippi,

Georgia and North Carolina produce most of the country's commercial sweet potato crop, along with hotter parts of California, Alabama and Arizona. Home gardeners are finding that new varieties of sweet potatoes don't take up much space, can be grown all over the country and are very productive. New varieties are highly pest resistant, and there is a great deal of interest in white sweet potatoes, which resemble common potatoes in taste and have more vitamin C than most tomatoes. Most important, more people are discovering the delectably rich, mellow quality of a fresh sweet potato, simply baked in its skin.

THE POTATO MUSEUM

BOX 791, GREAT FALLS, VA 22066, (703) 759-6714, IS OPEN BY APPOINTMENT ONLY. IT WAS MASTERMINDED BY E. THOMAS HUGHES WITH A COLLECTION OF POTATO ITEMS HE BEGAN ACQUIRING AS A GRADE-SCHOOL TEACHER IN BELGIUM. ONLY A SMALL PORTION OF THE COLLECTION IS ON DISPLAY AT ONCE. IT INCLUDES A POTATO-POWERED CLOCK, TOYS, AND JEWELRY MADE FROM POTATOES, LITERATURE ABOUT POTATOES INCLUDING SONGS AND JOKES, TOOLS FOR PLANTING AND COOKING SPUDS AND MANY OTHER ITEMS. HIS WIFE MEREDITH EDITS A MONTHLY MAGAZINE CALLED *PEELINGS*, WHICH IS INCLUDED AS PART OF THE ANNUAL MUSEUM MEMBERSHIP. THE COUPLE RECENTLY PUBLISHED A CHILDREN'S BOOK ON POTATOES.

Tuber Or Not Tuber

HOW POTATOES GROW

You don't have to know the difference between a chocolate chip and a silicon chip to write a letter on a computer or be able to distinguish an overhead cam shaft from getting the shaft in order to drive to the supermarket. Nor do you need a degree in botany to grow and harvest the most unforgettable-tasting potatoes ever. However, for your general edification here is a totally unexpurgated etymological and botanical analysis of the potato, plus a rudimentary explanation of the various potato parts.

A POTATO BY ANY OTHER NAME

First on the agenda is delving deeper into that murky underground where potatoes grow. For example, white potatoes are not exclusively white, nor did they originate in Ireland, despite their significant role in that country's culture and history. Also, sweet potatoes and white potatoes aren't even closely related. So who is what and what is who?

For lack of better names and to clarify the distinction, this book will use the terms common potato and sweet potato. The common potato is just one member of the multitudinous *Solanaceae*, or Nightshade family. With over ninety genera and some two thousand species, this family has every possible family archetype, from scapegoat poisons to hero medicinals, with many ornamental and food plants in between. Some of its other best-known members are tomato, pepper, eggplant, tobacco and petunia. Most are indigenous to both temperate and tropical regions of South and Central America. The genus *Solanum* itself has about seventeen hundred species, with the common potato being *Solanum tuberosum*.

Designated *Ipomoea batatas*, the sweet potato's genus is a group of merely five hundred or so species, most of which are ornamental, with the other well-known member being the morning glory. The silken bell-shaped flowers untwisting to the thunder of Helios's chariot provide the common name to the family *Convolvulaceae*. There are about fifty genera with some twelve hundred species of twining, succulent vines, shrubs and even trees, in the Morning Glory family, with most of them indigenous to tropical America or Asia.

As to the etymology of the word *potato* as well as other common names, grab your bag of chips, settle into the couch, and dig in.

In the Andes, the native people called the common potato *papas*, or tuber, with their descendants, the Quechua Indians, amassing over a thousand more names. Chilean natives called the wild tuber *malla* and the cultivated types *pogni*. The most obvious link between terms used by native populations and the Spanish invaders is the result of Columbus's confusing the common and the sweet potato, the latter of which was originally called *batata* in the West Indies. From that the Spanish derived *patata*, but in reference to the common potato. Confused yet? The Italians, who make the delicious gnocchi

POT HOLES

A TERM THAT ORIGINATED IN IRELAND, WHERE THE EARTH FLOOR IN THE HOME HAD A SHALLOW DEPRESSION TO HOLD THE POTATO POT, WHICH WAS PUSHED DOWN BY MASHING. IT WAS ALWAYS PUT IN THE SAME SPOT, WHICH GOT DEEPER OVER TIME.

pasta from potatoes, call them *patate*. In Greece, they are known as *patata*, and in Norway, *potet* or *potetes*, while the Swedish say *potatis*. The Spanish also referred to the new food as a "truffle" and an "earth apple." All these descriptives influenced the naming of the tuber in other countries.

> IN EUROPE, THE WATER THAT POTATOES HAVE BEEN BOILED IN IS USED AS A HEALING BALM FOR ACHES, SPRAINS AND BROKEN BONES. WASHING HEALTHY BODY PARTS IN IT WAS SUPPOSED TO CAUSE WARTS.

The truffle designation became the basis for many other names. The phrase *turma de terra* literally meant earth testicle. Though this name did not remain in use in Spain, the Italians adapted their names for truffles, *tartufi* and *tartufoli*, when they first used potatoes, which then became *tartuffo* and *tartuffolo*.

A French botanist, for reasons that remain obscure, changed the term to *cartoufle*, which turned into *kartoffel* in Germany. This term found wide use, with many variations including di-

minutives and nicknames, as the food gained popularity and became more commonly eaten. In Poland and Russia it was altered slightly to *kartofel*, and regional variations included *kartoska*, *kartopha*, *kartocla*, *kartova*, *karrofla*, *karcsofle*, and the Polish *taretofl*, Bulgarian *kartof*, Latvian *kartupelis*, and Serbian *krtola*.

Germans also used the term *erdapfel*, or earth apple, derivatives of which included *aardappel* in Holland and many versions of this in the numerous Dutch colonies in the Far East, like Malay and Ceylon, where they spoke of *artappels*. And, of course, the French use *pomme de terre*, though in early times, confusion was common about whether one was referring to potatoes or Jerusalem artichokes. *Truffes blanches* and *truffes rouges* are other old terms. The Welsh term for earth nut is *cloron*.

Many other names evolved all over the world. In Sanskrit, it is *alu*, while the Bengali say *bilati aloo*, or English tuber. Transylvanians called them *mere de pamint*, and the Finnish word is *maaomena*. Other earth apples are the Czech *zamnek*, the Polish *zemniak*, and the Ukrainian *zemnyak*, and the Persian *sib-I-zamini*.

batata

patata

patate

patata

potet

potatis

tartuffo

cartoufle

kartoffel

kartofel

kartof

kartupelis

krtola

erdapfel

aardappel

artappels

pomme de terre

cloron

alu

bilati aloo

mere de pamint

maaomena

zamnek

zemniak

zemnyak

sib-I-zamini

geo-melon

Modern Greeks use the term *geo-melon*.

The pear also was compared to the potato, and many names evolved from that connection. In German, pear was *birne* and in France *poire*. Germans called potatoes *grundbirne*. In Bavaria, this was altered to *krumbeer* and *krumpir* in Bulgaria. Serbians and Slovenians used the word *krompir*, and Lithuanians *klumberis*, while Hungarians said *krumpli* and Romanians *crumpira*.

An entirely different root stem from the southern Russian use of the Czech word for Brandenburg, *bramburk*, evolved into *mandyburka* or *gardyburka*. From the word *Brambor*, meaning Prussian, came the Romanian *brandraburca*, used as well as *carofla*.

Nicknames abound for potatoes, especially in countries where they are a staple food. Second to the Quechuas' thousand different names, the Irish probably have the most, with pratie possibly being the most common. Other slang terms include murphy and mickey, plus croker, taken from a popular variety there. In early times, the variety of potato one ate depended on social standing: the poor ate lumpers, while Gregor's cups were for the upper classes of Ireland. The Welsh originated the term taters.

The word spud is said to have come from Scotland or England, and referred to a spade or pronged fork used to dig potatoes. A "spuddy" was someone who sold bad potatoes. Another explanation for the term concerns a seventeenth-century group that thought the potato should be eliminated from the public's diet. They were called the Society for the Prevention of Unsatisfactory Diets, or S.P.U.D. The term is not one of endearment, regardless of the source.

Other derogatory expressions include potato-jaw, potato-trap, and potato-nose. And, of course, today we have couch potato.

Until around 1770, the term *potato* or some variation thereof was often used interchangeably with the common potato, the yam, and the sweet potato. Even now in the southern United States sweet potatoes are still regularly referred to as potatoes, while "Irish" potatoes are so designated. Confusion around sweet potatoes also began early on when Columbus first ate them in the West Indies and wrote that they looked like yams and tasted like chestnuts. African slaves called them *nyam* or *nyami*, most likely because they resembled the true yam (*Di-*

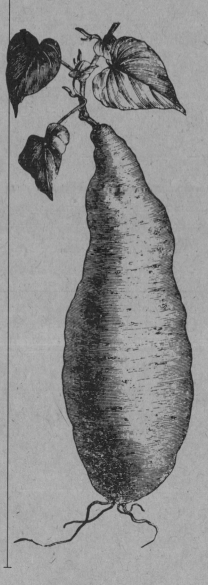

oscorea spp.), which grows in tropical areas around the world. The true yam is a vining plant, sometimes producing tubers up to six hundred pounds (273 kg). Once referred to as two-man, four-man, or six-man yams, to show how many deft males it took to lift one, today's true yams are seldom that large. Usually true yams are longer and more slender in shape than sweet potatoes and cannot be grown anywhere but in tropical climates.

Oddly, when sweet potatoes are deep orange in color and extrasweet in flavor, people are more likely to refer to them as yams, but in fact the true yam has a starchy, bland flavor.

ANATOMY OF A POTATO

The fruits of our labors, the common potato, further confounds and defies our use of the language by not actually being a fruit but rather a tuber. Even though they grow in the soil, tubers, to the uninitiated, are not true roots but rather the swollen tips of underground stems called rhizomes. These enlarged stems bear a supply of complex carbohydrates in the form of starches to ensure the availability of food for the plant in times of shortages.

The dimples that appear seemingly scattered but are actually spiraled about the circumference of the potato are the eyes. These are growth buds that can sprout

to reproduce a genetically identical plant. Sans cigar, the Groucho Marx eyebrow above each eye is a rudimentary leaf, imperfectly developed and nonfunctional, like an evolutionary appendix or wisdom tooth. The dots over the surface of the potato are called lenticels, and they allow the skin to breathe. More lenticels are found on the aboveground stems of the potato plant.

If you dissect a potato, you will find a core, called the inner medulla, or pith. This has side branches extending to each eye. When planting common potatoes, some gardeners cut their seed potatoes along these lines, including parts of these veins, and particularly the main vein, in each seed piece. The outer medulla is the main fleshy portion of the potato. These various structures are most

600 POUNDS

easily seen in pink or blue common potatoes.

Surrounding the inner and outer medulla is a vascular ring. Protecting this is the cortex, then the corky epidermis, and finally the periderm layer.

Tubers attach to the main stems of the plant via thinner underground stems. Finer-textured, vertically growing true roots extend from the original seed piece, the main stems, and along the thinner underground stems. With most potato varieties, the new tubers develop from the stem above the original seed piece.

> ## "HE COULD FIDDLE ALL THE BUGS OFF A SWEET POTATO-VINE."
>
> **Stephen Vincent Benet**
> *The Mountain Whippoorwill*

The upper part of a potato plant is a conventional composite of stems, leaves and flowers. With common potatoes, the thick, succulent, floppy yet generally upright stems can grow to about three feet (91.5 cm). Crinkly, dark green leaves, divided into pairs of leaflets, may measure up to ten inches (25 cm) long.

Clusters of star-shaped, usually white to blue-white

CROSS SECTION OF TUBER

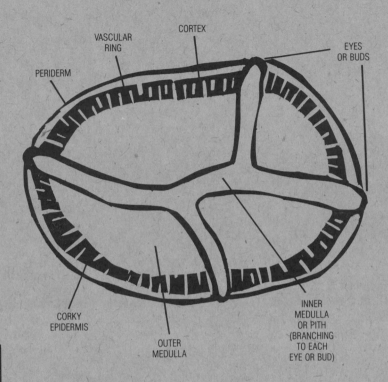

VASCULAR RING

CORTEX

PERIDERM

EYES OR BUDS

CORKY EPIDERMIS

OUTER MEDULLA

INNER MEDULLA OR PITH (BRANCHING TO EACH EYE OR BUD)

flowers, one inch (2.5 cm) across, are centered with bright yellow stamens. Never likely to compete with roses or orchids, they still have their charm—witness the results of French potato promoter Antoine-Augustin Parmentier. To gain favor for his beloved potato, he presented Louis XVI a bouquet of potato flowers on the King's thirty-first birthday, August 23, 1785. Obligingly, the king tucked one into his lapel, and more were tucked into the wig of Marie Antoinette, a sure sign of favor.

When a flower is pollinated, a tomato-like fruit develops, three-quarters of an inch (2 cm) across, which is toxic and therefore inedible, like the entire upper portion of the plant.

Sweet potatoes are tuberous, or tuber-like—true roots rather than tubers. Their stems are trailing vines, usually to about four feet (122 cm) long. The smooth, shiny six-inch (15 cm) leaves may be oval or lobed. Rose-violet to pale pink, the morning glory-like flowers are two inches (5 cm) long.

GUESS WHAT'S COMING FOR DINNER?

THIS PIECE OF POTATO FOLKLORE RELATES TO A TRAIT CHARACTERISTIC OF THE SOLANACEAE, OR NIGHTSHADE FAMILY—THE PRESENCE OF THE ALKALOID SOLANINE (AND TO A LESSER EXTENT CHACONINE).

IN THIS STORY, QUEEN ELIZABETH I WAS PRESENTED WITH SOME POTATO PLANTS. THE QUEEN'S COOKS DISPENSED WITH THE KNOBBY TUBERS AND PROCEEDED TO BOIL THE STEMS AND LEAVES, WHICH HAVE THE HIGHEST AMOUNTS OF ALKALOIDS. NEEDLESS TO SAY, EVERYONE PRESENTLY BECAME VIOLENTLY ILL, THEREBY DELAYING ACCEPTANCE OF THE VEGETABLE FOR SEVERAL CENTURIES. POTATO TUBERS HAVE VERY SMALL AMOUNTS OF THE ALKALOIDS, AND THEY ACTUALLY CONTRIBUTE TO THEIR GOOD FLAVOR. ONLY WHEN EXPOSED TO LIGHT OR EXTREME HOT OR COLD TEMPERATURES IN STORAGE DO THE TUBERS ACCUMULATE TO TOXIC LEVELS. THIS IS EASY TO SPOT IN THE CASE OF LIGHT, AS IT TURNS THE TUBER GREEN. IT IS ALSO AN ARGUMENT FOR PEELING POTATOES, AS THE ALKALOIDS CONCENTRATE IN THE POTATO'S OUTER SURFACE.

THE GREAT POTATO PLOT

SELECTING AND PREPARING A SITE

It's no mystery that potatoes are beautiful garden plants. If you need precedent, look to the gardeners of the Spanish and English Renaissance courts who esteemed the common potato's appearance enough to include them in pots and formal flower beds. Closer to home, as it were, one need only drive about the countryside, peering across lawns and fences into backyards, to see large vegetable gardens, the lushest, prettiest part of which is the potato portion. Luxuriant mounds, two- to three-feet (61 to 91.5 cm) tall, of verdant foliage with twinkling white stars peeking out shyly, this plant is no small fry. The sweet potato's exuberant vines spread nattily along as a ground cover or cascade gracefully over the sides of containers or walls.

Potatoes are also among the most productive of garden plants, equalled only by tomatoes and carrots. A ten-foot-square (3 m) plot can produce eighty to one hundred pounds (36 to 45.5 kg) in only a few months.

The potato's tragic flaw is that the plants of common potatoes yellow and wither unattractively before harvesting—not exactly what most people want in their flower beds by the terrace, but potatoes do have their place in a well-designed kitchen garden. The choice is yours; there are still sweet potatoes to wend their magic about the patio.

In deciding what role you want potatoes to play in your overall landscape design as well as the food producing portion of your garden, you'll have to consider the "optimal site." These words of course strike terror into the heart of every potential gardener. Who among you has not just signed a thirty-year mortgage for a postage stamp lot, and then had a garden writer tell you in no uncertain terms that the plant you've been wanting to grow for years needs a specific climate, light and soil that differ radically from what you can provide?

Never fear. While there are optimum conditions for growing potatoes successfully, there is also a great deal of latitude. People have been known to grow ample quantities of potatoes in a pit of leaf mold; on bare rock with seaweed heaped over them; beneath piles of hay and straw; or in a windrow of rotting leaves, weeds, clippings and manure. Here then are the broad brush strokes of that best of all possible worlds, to be modified as time, temperament and conditions necessitate.

CLIMATE

Naturally growing in mountainous climates to heights of about fifteen thousand feet (4,572 m), or roughly the equivalent of halfway up

> SINCE 1966, THE CONSUMPTION OF FRESH VERSUS PROCESSED COMMON POTATOES IN THE UNITED STATES HAS REVERSED WITH 77 POUNDS (35 KG) PROCESSED AND 47 POUNDS (21.5 KG) FRESH USED BY THE AVERAGE PERSON EACH YEAR IN THE UNITED STATES.

Mount Everest, the common potato is accustomed to cooler temperatures. Most commercial production is located in places like Maine, Washington, North Dakota, and, of course, Idaho. Ideal conditions for tuber development are short days, temperatures between 60° and 70°F. (16° and 21°C.) and average moisture and fertility. Tubers do not form when temperatures are above 80°F. (27°C.). Conditions opposite those above promote aboveground growth instead of tubers.

raised beds or containers, under plastic tunnels, or in a greenhouse.

LIGHT

Both common and sweet potatoes need a garden location with full sunlight or at least a minimum of six hours of sun a day. Morning sun is cooler, so a location with it would be good for common potatoes in the South; a site with hot afternoon sun would be good for growing sweet potatoes in the north.

SOIL

Gone are the days when one would select a homesite for the soil it offered. A great many other priorities logically take precedent. Fortunately, a number of relative painless alternative growing methods offer either short- or long-term solutions

Still, gardeners in much of the country grow potatoes. One way they compensate is to select varieties proven to grow well in their area. Another way is to grow potatoes in the coolest times of the year, and, if necessary, harvest all the potatoes as "new" ones before hot weather sets in. The farther south one lives, the earlier one can plant, with January through April the usual time span and some people planting as early as November.

Tropical native sweet potatoes present the opposite dilemma. They are highly heat tolerant and thrive in the Deep South with its long,

hot, humid growing periods. They are also frost sensitive, with even the lightest frost destroying leaves, and soil temperatures of 50°F. (10°C.) damaging the roots. Areas with months of mean daily temperatures of 70°F. (21°C.) are necessary for commercial production, such as the Deep South, as well as the hottest regions of Arizona and California.

Even so, sweet potatoes are grown well into the far North and even in cool, mild climates such as the Pacific Northwest by selecting varieties with a short growing season, mulching with black plastic or growing them in

to less than ideal soil.

Short-term solutions include growing in containers, potato barrels, tire or chicken wire towers, raised beds or thick organic mulches. These methods are all described in detail in Chapter 5. Long-term solutions involve taking a close look at your soil and adjusting and modifying the mineral content, pH and organic matter content over a period of years.

Although a deep sandy or silty loam is the technical terminology for the ideal potato soil, the key is having plenty of well-decayed organic matter, good drainage, few weeds, and loose, well-tilled soil with few large lumps, clods or rocks to inhibit tuber development.

Healthy soil is an ideal balance of inorganic particles of sand, silt and clay in combination with decaying organic materials referred to as humus. A balance of air and water is also necessary in soil. Gardening is not an exact science, and, as mentioned earlier, plants always allow us a certain amount of latitude. In this case, a range of proportions of these elements will produce healthy plants and abundant crops. Experience is the best teacher, so don't be afraid to garden and learn from less than overwhelming success.

One way to find out about your soil is to have it tested. Most gardeners use their Co-operative Extension Service to analyze their soils. Private labs are also available, and many will give a more comprehensive report, although they charge higher fees. In some locales, garden supply stores offer this service to

NASA WILL TRY GROWING POTATOES IN OUTER SPACE AS SOON AS A VARIETY THAT IS ADAPTABLE TO THE SIXTEEN- TO TWENTY-HOUR GROWING DAY IS FOUND. ALONG WITH WHEAT AND SOYBEANS, POTATOES WILL BE TESTED AS A FOOD SOURCE THAT CAN BE GROWN BY SPACE TRAVELLERS.

their customers. Excellent home soil test kits are also available. Most labs and kits provide guidelines for collecting samples from your garden.

What will these tests tell you? Generally, you get infor-

TRUE TEMPER

IDAHO POTATOES

mation about the soil type, pH, organic matter content, and the levels of nitrogen, phosphorus and potassium as well as other major and minor nutrients. Recommendations are made concerning supplements needed.

SOIL TYPE

A quick way to determine your soil type is turn up a spadeful of soil three to five days after a rainfall, take a small handful, and squeeze it into a ball. Open your fist. Does the ball keep its shape? You've got a soil high in clay. A sandy soil readily breaks apart and feels gritty. If the ball crumbles loosely, it's a silty loam.

SOIL DRAINAGE

Test drainage by digging a hole six inches (15 cm) wide and twelve inches (30.5 cm) deep, filling it with water, letting it drain, and immediately filling it again. This second time note how long it takes to drain. If more than eight hours elapse, you've got poorly draining soil. If it's just a matter of it being a clay soil, adding organic matter will help, but if the poor drainage is due to an impervious layer beneath the top-soil, then the answer is drainage tiles, raised beds or growing in containers.

SOIL pH

The pH of a soil indicates its acidity or alkalinity. It is measured on a scale of 0 to 14; with 7 being neutral, 7.1 and higher being alkaline, and 6.9 and lower being acid. Most soils are usually slightly acid to neutral, which is also the ideal range for the preponderance of plants. The importance of pH is that it affects the intake of nutrients from soil by the plants.

With common potatoes, there is also a secondary effect. At a pH of 5.7 or lower, the potato disease called scab is kept to a minimum, because it can't thrive in acid soil. A pH of 5.2 to 6.0 is the tolerance range for common potatoes. Sweet potatoes grow well in a range from 5.6 to 6.8.

To lower soil pH, the most often used material is agricultural sulfur. Unfortunately, there is no simple rule for

adding sulfur that will work in all cases. A general recommendation to lower the pH by one unit is to add one pound (.5 kg) of sulfur per one hundred square feet (31 m), mixing it into the top three or four inches (8 or 10 cm) of soil.

To raise soil pH, ground calcitic or dolomitic limestone is used, with calcitic

> THE PUREE POTATOES, WHICH HE WOULD HAVE CALLED MASHED, WERE LIKE NO MASHED POTATOES HE HAD EVER SAMPLED . . . IF ANGELS EVER ATE MASHED POTATOES THEY WOULD CALL ON PELLEW'S CHEF TO PREPARE THEM.
>
> *Hornblower and the Hotspur*, 1962
> C. S. Forester

preferred unless the soil is magnesium deficient. Again, initial pH and soil type affect the amount needed, but a guideline is five pounds (2.5 kg) per one hundred square feet (31 m) to raise the pH by one point, with sandy soils needing less and clay soils needing more.

PLANT NUTRITION AND ORGANIC MATTER

Plants make their own food by photosynthesis, but certain raw materials are necessary, with most absorbed from water in the soil through the roots up into the plant. Sixteen of these elements are essential for plant growth. The elements necessary in large quantities, called macronutrients, are carbon, hydrogen, oxygen, nitrogen, phosphorus, potassium, calcium, magnesium and sulfur. The micronutrients are boron, chlorine, copper, iron, manganese, molybdenum and zinc.

Air and water provide the carbon, hydrogen and oxygen. The elements needed in the largest quantity and most often supplemented by man are nitrogen, phosphorus and potassium. A bag or box of fertilizer will have three numbers, such as 5-10-10, which indicates the percentage of these three elements, in

respective order. The other macro- and micronutrients are usually sufficient in most garden soils, but soil tests will let you know of potential problems.

Because plants absorb the essential nutrients in their most elemental form in the water found in the soil, the source of these nutrients can be either from synthetic fertilizers or from natural plant and animal materials or from mined rock minerals. Although soluble chemical

fertilizers seemed like a panacea when first developed, they have proven otherwise. Besides being synthesized from nonrenewable resources, chemical fertilizers do not enrich the soil's organic matter content, which is necessary for beneficial soil microorganisms and earthworms as well as for maintaining soil structure and water-holding capacity.

In addition to contributing nutrients to the soil, organic matter and fertilizers loosen

soil structure, help retain water in the soil while at the same time improving drainage, increase microorganism and earthworm activity in the soil and help decrease plant pest problems. Homemade compost—recycling plant waste into a usable soil conditioner and fertilizer—is the ideal solution, but we can't always make enough of it for all our gardening needs. What are the alternatives?

There are many new "natural" and "organic" fertilizers on the market today. But what are they? Don't buy one unless you know what is in the bag, as it might contain something you would not choose to put in your garden. As far as the fertilizer industry is concerned, the term *organic* can describe anything containing carbon and one or more elements essential for plant growth. Theoretically, "natural"

should be anything derived from a plant, animal or mineral, but it's an ambiguous designation. Until stricter guidelines are developed and enforced, we gardeners must look out for ourselves and our soil.

Groups who certify organic produce have guidelines, but each state has different items allowed or prohibited. The listing of the three numbers on the bag is all that is officially required. Actual sources of the ingredients do not have to be included. Organic materials with low solubility do not have high numbers on bags because their nutrition is generally available less quickly than the nutrition from chemical sources. "Organic" fertilizers with high numbers are usually standard chemical formulas with organic matter added for bulk. Your best bet is to buy locally composted organic materials, if you must buy at all. Simply adding composted manure every year

to your soil will add humus and meet most plant needs. Buying premixed, "complete" (containing nitrogen, phosphorus and potassium) fertilizers is a risky but viable alternative.

An interesting at-home test of any fertilizer or fertilizer component is suggested by Bill Wolf, president of Necessary Trading Company, which distributes organic products: Offer a sample to some earthworms. If they head for it, it's probably okay. If they run, you should, too.

Another option is to mix your own organic fertilizer. In and of themselves, very few materials provide enough nutrition in the right balance. But by combining several different materials, you can develop a complete general-purpose organic fertilizer specifically tailored to your garden. Be sure that the material is not full of toxic pesticides or other contaminants, as much cottonseed meal is, except for the feed-

> **LONG USED BY FARMERS AS PIG FEED, POTATOES AND THEIR PEELS ARE NOURISHING AND FILLING ADDITIONS TO THE DIETS OF MANY LIVESTOCK ANIMALS. OFTEN DEHYDRATED POTATO PRODUCTS ARE UTILIZED FOR ANIMAL FOOD.**

grade type. For example, to get nitrogen, use two parts blood meal or three parts fish, feather, alfalfa, soybean or cottonseed meal; for phosphorus, add three parts bonemeal or six parts rock phosphate or colloidal phosphate; for potassium, one part kelp meal or six parts greensand.

Application rates depend on your soil's fertility combined with the needs of your potatoes. You can usually add five to ten pounds (2.5 to 5 kg) of organic fertilizer per hundred square feet (31 m) without overfertilizing. Too much nitrogen fertilizer causes both common and sweet potatoes to produce abundant top growth at the expense of the potatoes themselves. Healthy soil that's been built up over a period of years with annual additions of compost and other organic matter will often not even need additional fertilizer at planting time.

SOIL PREPARATION

Plan ahead. For those breaking new ground for potatoes, try to decide in the autumn where you want to plant potatoes the following spring. Till or dig your bed as deeply as possible, removing rocks and incorporating organic matter such as compost or

composted manure. The action of freezing and thawing over the winter will loosen the soil and make it better for plant growth and tuber development.

If you already have a vegetable garden area established, it will probably be adequate, unless you haven't been adding organic matter. Dig or till at least a two-inch thick (5 cm) layer of compost or composted manure into the soil a month before planting.

ROTATION AND COMPANION PLANTING

Although it is not imperative to grow potatoes in a different part of the garden every year—a practice known as rotation—it is advisable. Sooner or later, you'll pay a high price for neglecting this commonsense method of minimizing plant pests and encouraging healthy plant growth. There are several reasons for rotating crops in the food garden. Many pests are troublesome only to a certain plant or family of plants. By avoiding planting the same plants or family members in the same place year after year, the pests have no hosts and populations are kept in check. Weed control is improved too. A niche is

CURES AND SUPERSTITIONS

Potatoes were used as a cure for scurvy. Appropriate, as they were (and still are) high in vitamin C and are stored better than citrus on long sea voyages.

provided for certain weeds with each different crop. Eradicating these weeds can be aided by rotating plants with different methods of cultivation. Rotating plants also keeps nutrients in balance. Root crops are light feeders, while leaf and fruiting crops are heavy feeders. Legumes like peas and beans add nitrogen to the soil but need lots of phosphorus. Adding a

green manure crop, such as buckwheat or clover, to the cycle improves the soil and discourages certain pests.

Common potatoes have proven to yield best after corn, winter rye, winter wheat, sweet clover or soybeans, with soybeans helping to decrease the incidence of scab. If peas, oats, or barley precede potatoes, scab increases. Potatoes, peppers, tomatoes and eggplants should not be planted in the same space more often than once every three years. For sweet potatoes, wait three years before planting again in the same spot. Again, this keeps soilborne diseases from thriving.

Companion planting is a method full of traditional lore and beliefs. Often defying scientific substantiation, it is a

commonly accepted practice around the world. Different plants, grown in proximity to one another, may provide shade, relief from winds, keep soil loose, inhibit weeds, repel insects, attract insect enemies or provide some undefinable benefit. Gardeners have found that beans, corn, cabbage, lettuce, petunias, and radishes are good companions for potato plants. Avoid planting potatoes near apples, pumpkins, raspberries, squash and tomatoes.

Potatoes may hinder the growth of cucumbers and spinach. Horseradish, onions, catnip and coriander deter potato beetles. Eggplant is preyed upon by many of the same pests as potatoes, and so can be a sacrifice crop. Biodynamic gardeners rely on pigweed to strengthen potato plants and improve the flavor of the tubers. Potatoes planted in squash hills may prevent squash bugs; the potatoes are sacrificial as they will not produce much with all the squash foliage.

Potato Troubleshooting
Soil Problems

Common Potatoes

Adding fresh manure to soil can
result in scab.

Small potatoes can be the result of soil
that is too
alkaline, has too much nitrogen,
or is low in phosophorus or potassium.

Lush foliage but no potatoes may be from
too much nitrogen in the soil.

Sweet Potatoes

Long, stringy or poorly formed tubers
result from heavy or wet soil or a
potassium deficiency.

Delayed maturity or long, skinny tubers
result from a combination of excessive
nitrogen and water.

Small potatoes and lush top growth
often result from too much nitrogen or soil
that is heavily clay.

Recommended Organic Fertilizers

Following are some of the complete organic fertilizers produced from contaminant-free sources:

Agway Nature's Way Organic Plant Food

All Natural Organic Flower and Garden Food

Baa Baa Doo

Compostost

Door County 100% Organic Fish Compost

Fertilaid

Green Earth Organics Natural Fertilizer

Greenview Certified for Flowers and Vegetables

Naturall Organic Natural Fertilizer for Gardens

Nature's Best All Natural Organic Garden Fertilizer

Nature's Choice Organic Garden Fertilizer

Necessary Starter Fertilizer

Plant Right All Natural Organic Fertilizer

Pure-Tex

Ringer Vegetable Garden Restore

Sustane

Zoo Doo

FOUR

The Eyes Have It

PREPARING "SEED" POTATOES AND SLIPS

Potatoes are not usually planted from actual seeds. Instead, a piece of tuber, called a "seed potato," with one or more potato eyes that one hopes will sprout and form a new plant, is buried in the soil. Slips, usually used for planting sweet potatoes, are the small plants that sprout from each eye.

What about the flowers and berries resembling small green tomatoes that one sometimes sees on the potato plant itself? Poisonous and *never* to be consumed, these berries do indeed contain seeds. They are the result of pollination and produce offspring that are not identical to the parents. Only when this pollination is controlled, and sometimes not even then, will the use of seeds produce uniform potatoes. For plant breeders, this genetic diversity has the potential for introducing important traits, such as improved flavor, growth or disease resistance.

Horticulturists have experimented with the seeds and achieved mixed results. So tiny that fifty thousand make an ounce, potato seeds are best started indoors and later transferred to the garden, where they may or may not produce a crop of decent-sized potatoes the first year. If not, the tubers can be planted the next year. What growing potatoes from true seed accomplishes is avoidance of tuber-borne diseases and cold-weather tilling. Of the four or so varieties currently available, the hybrid 'Homestead' offers the most uniform, rapid growth and significant yields in about three months from transplanting outdoors. Seed potatoes, on the other hand, produce exact duplicates of themselves. The sprout arising from a seed potato is genetically identical to the tuber from which it arises.

There are many schools of thought when it comes to preparing seed potatoes and sweet potato slips. Arguments rage among gardeners growing common potatoes about using whole potatoes or pieces, large or small, healed over or not, dusted with sulfur or not, presprouted or not, home-grown or purchased. If you're looking for

> THE ANNUAL POTATO BLOSSOM FESTIVAL IN AROOSTOOK COUNTY, MAINE, FEATURES MASHED-POTATO WRESTLING, A PARADE, AND, OF COURSE, A POTATO BLOSSOM QUEEN.

hard-and-fast rules, stick out your thumb and head for another planet. Ours is a world of choices. I can give you information about the various methods, and nudge you in the directions that offer the greatest probability of success.

WHOLE OR PIECES, LARGE OR SMALL

Most gardeners and seed companies advise using small potatoes, less than two inches (5 cm), known as "B"-size tubers, whole. Some growers prefer large potatoes cut into pieces the size of a golf ball, small hen's egg, or large ice cube, weighing about one and one-half to two ounces (42.5 to 57 g). Yet others cut up

their large tubers into even smaller cubes, making sure that two or even three eyes are included on each section. Large potatoes are not recommended for planting whole.

The thinking behind larger versus smaller pieces is that a larger piece seems to survive more readily. They have more energy and resilience, and the young early-season plants are more likely to thrive, especially when early spring conditions are less than ideal. They also seem to withstand injury better than smaller ones. The size of the seed piece also affects the potato crop itself. Generally, larger seed pieces produce high yields of small- to medium-sized potatoes. Small seed

pieces lead to lower yields of larger tubers.

Some seed companies or individuals try to get as many seed potatoes per tuber as possible, with each piece having only one eye. Although satisfactory results are possible, having multiple eyes improves production per plant by generating multiple sprouts, but this, too, affects tuber size and yield. If one sprout dies, it is likely that the others will still grow well. With little stored food to sustain them, smaller seed potatoes, whether from cut pieces or the tissue-culture spud buds (explained later), most readily produce a normal crop if precautions are made to plant them less deeply than bigger pieces and when the soil is above 50°F. (10°C.).

When you cut the potato pieces yourself, take care to use a clean, sharp knife. Avoid any chance of contamination from piece to piece by dipping the blade in rubbing alcohol or diluted household bleach between each cut.

TAKING THE CURE
Curing a potato is a means of letting the cut surface of seed potato pieces heal over, or suberize. In the suberization process a waxy, waterproof substance called suberin

develops in the cell walls, causing them to become corky. These pieces retain their moisture when planted, yet resist diseases that cause rotting. The majority of gardeners favor healing over, feeling better safe than sorry. But the U.S. Department of Agriculture gardening publications urge cutting immediately before planting, with the attitude that moisture loss weakens the piece and that rot organisms can take over during the curing period. The deciding factor is suiting the method to the conditions. If the soil is on the cool side when you are

> **BOILING A POT OF POTATOES AND DUMPING THEM ON THE NEIGHBOR'S FIELD WAS THOUGHT TO DESTROY HIS CROP.**

planting, most experts agree that healing over is wise. Wet soil is another reason to heal over the cut pieces. To cure, or heal over, potato pieces, spread them out on a newspaper in a bright, well-ventilated place at about 70°F. (21°C.) with high humidity for twenty-four hours. The surface will feel slightly dry and hardened.

> "OH, THE PRATIES
> THEY ARE SMALL—
> OVER HERE, OVER
> HERE.
> OH, THE PRATIES
> THEY ARE SMALL
> WHEN WE DIG 'EM IN
> THE FALL,
> AND WE EAT 'EM,
> COATS AND ALL,
> FULL OF FEAR, FULL
> OF FEAR."
>
> Irish Famine Song, 1846–47
> Anonymous

A SULFUROUS SITUATION

In areas with rainy springs, dusting the cut seed potato pieces with a fungicide like sulfur is a simple way to prevent disease problems early in the season. A cheap, natural fungicide, agricultural sulfur or flowers of can be purchased at most drugstores, and it takes only a few ounces to dust ten pounds (5 kg) of seed potatoes. The method is simple: Put the seed pieces in a paper bag with a bit of powdered sulfur and shake. The pieces are removed and cured as above or planted immediately. Another rot preventative is to dip cut pieces into a diluted solution of household bleach. Purchased seed potato pieces are often already dusted with sulfur. Small whole seed potatoes do not need dusting.

SPROUTING OFF

Who among you hasn't left some potatoes under the sink, only to notice a rotten smell one day, then upon opening the door seen something looking like long bony fingers reaching out to grab you? Voilà! Potato sprouts. Planting sprouted seed potatoes rather than dormant ones is usually an advantage, especially with early potatoes. It is especially recommended for gardeners in more northern climates with late frosts and wet soil to ensure an adequate growing season and an abundant crop.

Given how easily the under-sink potato monsters grow, specific directions may be overkill, but for the best possible sprouts proceed as follows. Two to four weeks before planting time, take whole potatoes and place the ends with the greatest number of eyes uppermost on a tray. Set the tray in a light, but not bright, room with a daytime temperature of 60°F. to 70°F. (16° to 21°C.). The tubers should start growing and produce short, stubby shoots (about one-eighth of an inch in length), which are preferable to long and scraggly ones. It is important to not damage these sprouts when the tubers get cut up for planting. One way to encour-age sprouting is to put potatoes in a paper bag with an ethylene gas-producing banana or apple for several days.

The number of sprouts on each seed potato influences yields. With only one sprout, the crop will be small but tubers large. With two sprouts, you'll get a lot of big potatoes plus some average-sized ones. Starting with three sprouts, the crop will be mainly large and medium ones, but also many small potatoes. Both dormant tubers and tubers with four or more sprouts yield mainly small potatoes. An unusual twist on the sprouting scheme is to pull off the sprouts when they are four to six inches (10 to 15 cm) long and plant them with just the tip at the soil surface. The seed potatoes are allowed to produce another one or two sets, each pulled off and planted as before. Finally, the potatoes are cut up and planted.

Certified seed stock has been inspected during growth and storage to be disease-free. Using certified seed can be the single most important factor in successful potato growing year after year. On the other hand, using potatoes from your own garden is a step toward self-sufficiency and ensures that a particular strain remains alive. But, even plants that look healthy can pick up a virus from insects, with the disease gaining strength when tubers are replanted, leaving a diseased crop. The best solution is probably a compromise. Regularly buying certified stock enables you to have a dependable supply of potatoes. Replanting a portion from your own stock gives you some autonomy.

One mistake beginning potato gardeners often make is assuming that they can plant tubers from the grocery store.

HIGH-TECH TATERS

The latest twist on seed potatoes is tiny tubers from marble size to about one inch (2.5 cm) in diameter that are produced via a laboratory technique called tissue culture. Sold as spud buds or minitubers, these are state-of-the-art disease-free. Like regular seed potatoes, each is genetically the same as the original. They are planted whole, set about two to four inches (5 to 10 cm) deep and 18 inches (46 cm) apart, and produce about three pounds (1.5 kg) of potatoes each. Fewer than a dozen varieties are available.

A POTATO SAVED

Whether you buy certified seed potatoes each year or save and use seed potatoes from your own garden is a decision with a double edge.

POTATO CLOCK

INSTEAD OF BATTERIES, TWO POTATOES POWER A DIGITAL TIME KEEPER. THEY MUST BE REPLACED BEFORE THEY SPOIL.

Often these have been treated with chemicals to prevent sprouting, plus they are likely not to be the best variety for your garden, even if they do sprout.

Dedicated grow-your-own gardeners like the notion of continuing their own seed stock. They select small- to medium-sized, well-shaped, scab-free tubers with no fissures or corky blemishes to use the following season. Drying potatoes in the sun and brushing off the soil after harvesting is important, but washing is not a good idea. Gardeners in southern areas should be careful to avoid sunscald when drying potatoes. Like the food crop, these seed potatoes must be stored in a well-ventilated root cellar with high humidity (80 to 90 percent) and cool temperatures of 35° to 40°F (2° to 5°C). More casually inclined gardeners cull what is left from their food crop in early spring and plant the best of it.

An unorthodox means of saving seed potatoes actually seems logical to anyone who has noticed the occasional volunteer potato plants that sprout from potatoes missed in the previous autumn harvest. In other words, simply replant a portion of the harvest immediately in the autumn. Potato tubers will

overwinter to at least −20°F. (−29°C.), depending on snow cover, mulching and freezing and thawing.

Your slip is showing
A planting of sweet potatoes is started from what are called slips, or sprouts with leaves, and sometimes roots, that grow from sweet potatoes. Slips are usually sold in bunches of twenty-five or fifty at garden centers in the spring or bought from mail-order sources, who ship them at the best planting time. As with common potatoes, certified disease-free sweet potato slips or tuberous roots are your best insurance against

FOR PREVENTING RHEUMATISM, A DRIED PIECE OF POTATO WAS HUNG AROUND THE NECK IN A BAG OR CARRIED IN A POCKET.

disease problems in the garden.

Sweet potato slips rival those air plants sold at state fairs for resiliency. Even if the newly arrived slips look wilted and near death, they are usually going to be fine as soon as they are planted. One way to help them along is to immerse the roots in a jar of water and put a plastic bag

over the leaves. Within several days, new growth starts.

If you grew a sweet potato crop last year or have a neighbor who did, you can use some of the best-shaped, blemish-free roots to grow your own sprouts in the spring. As with common potatoes, the grocery store is not a good source for starting sweet potatoes.

To make sure your plants don't carry stem-rot disease, before harvesting cut or slit the crown and underground stems and check for dark streaks or blotches. Also,

don't use any sweet potatoes with surface cracks or darkened eyes, which indicate nematode infestation.

To start your own slips, you'll need about one sweet potato for every dozen plants you want to grow. You can make the slip-starting procedure as easy or as difficult as you'd like. The easiest is to half submerge a sweet potato vertically in a jar or glass of water, holding it at the proper height with that low-tech method remembered from your days of starting avocado seeds, that is, strategically

placed toothpicks. Place it in a warm, sunny window. To move a little upscale, take a shallow pot (the garden variety, not a cooking pot) and fill it with moist potting soil or sand, then horizontally sink a sweet potato halfway in. Within weeks either method will yield leafy shoots, which are carefully broken off and planted into the garden when six to twelve inches (15 to 30.5 cm) tall. Those started in the sand are most likely to have roots, but the sprouts from the water-grown potato can be simply broken off and planted directly in the garden or placed in another jar of water for roots to develop before planting out.

If you're into either form or quantity, sweet potato slips can be started in a cold frame filled with sand and a heating cable. Plant tubers lengthways to half their depth.

WHAT I SAY IS, THAT IF A MAN REALLY LIKES POTATOES, HE MUST BE A PRETTY DECENT SORT OF FELLOW.

Not That It Matters
A. A. Milne

How Much, How Many?

WHEN DETERMINING HOW MUCH SPACE
YOU WANT TO ALLOCATE
AND HOW MANY SEED POTATOES
OR SLIPS TO BUY OR START,
USE THE FOLLOWING GUIDELINES:

COMMON POTATOES
10 TO 12 POUNDS (4.5 TO 5.5 KG)
OF SEED POTATOES ARE NECESSARY
TO PLANT 100 FEET OF ROW,
WHICH WILL YIELD 80 TO 100 POUNDS
(36 TO 45.5 KG) OF POTATOES.

SWEET POTATOES
24 SLIPS WILL PLANT A
25-FOOT (7.5 M) ROW
AND YIELD 60 TO 75 POUNDS
(27 TO 34 KG) OF EDIBLE ROOTS.

POTATO PRINTING

Just as in the kitchen where the potato may be simply boiled or done up as a duchess, so, too, the potato can serve as an art medium for anyone from toddlers to highly skilled adults. Possessed of a large, smooth, easily carved surface, the potato has long been a natural for block printing.

Armed with temperas and rolls of paper, children can create designs and patterns for their own pleasure or to use as handmade gift wrap. Upgrade the paint to gilt, the paper to handmade, and the evolution to elegant is complete. Stamp pads, water-soluble printing ink, acrylic paint and colorfast dyes are other more permanent options.

On what can you make an impression? Just about any flat surface. Besides trim around windows, ceilings and doors, consider placemats, tablecloths, dish towels, pot holders, window shades, curtains and lamp shades for your home. Or, make gift tags, note cards and gift bags in addition to wrapping paper. Clothing takes to potato printing, whether T-shirts, sweatshirts, skirts, dresses, beach cover-ups or aprons.

The materials needed for potato printing include, of course, one or more large, firm potatoes, a pocket or paring knife, a garbage bag or other large piece of plastic, old newspaper, paint or ink, china plates and artist's brushes for mixing paint.

Cut the potato in half and carve a design on the surface, cutting away everything you don't want to be colored. Spread out plastic and newspapers on the work surface. Mix paint, using a different plate for each color. Use a brush to spread the paint out on the plate, adding a bit of water if necessary to thin the paint. Lightly dip the potato into the paint or onto an ink pad, then apply it to your surface. Repeat as desired and allow to dry before using the item.

FIVE

Plant One On Me, Baby

CONVENTIONAL AND UNUSUAL WAYS OF PLANTING POTATOES

Making allowances for variations on a theme, gardeners can essentially be delineated into two basic types. One is the by-the-book, it's-always-been-done-this-way, straight-rows-forever type who blanches at the mention of a porous-hose irrigation system, raised bed or protective fabric row cover. The other is the Rube Goldberg type who eagerly tries out every new gadget, gizmo or growing method. Twirling composters, foot-thick mulches, double-wall cold frames, and new strains of *Bacillus* makes this gardener's heart skip beats. The most obvious deviation within this second group is between the doers and the buyers, or those who want to make everything themselves and those who reverently read garden supply catalogues on Sunday mornings before, or even instead of, *The New York Times*.

When ready to plant potatoes, you most likely will find yourself naturally drifting into one of these two general directions. There are the safe, conservative planting times and methods, and there are the techniques that stretch seasons and incredulity. Potatoes are Zen enough

to respond serenely to all comers with a fullness of spirit and growth.

THE BEST OF TIMES

Flourishing in cool temperatures and needing ninety to one hundred twenty frost-free growing days to reach full maturity, common potatoes are planted as early in the spring as possible. The earliest planting is made anytime from six weeks to just before the last killing frost. The soil should be dry enough to be worked and about 45°F. (7°C.). If sprouts get frosted, there is usually new growth to replace them. The main crop is best planted one hundred twenty days before the autumn's first killing frost and when the soil is at least 50°F. (10°C.).

For northern areas, this means planting from April to mid-June. In the southern and warmer western regions, planting can begin at least as early as January, if not before, and up through March or April, then again in July through September for an autumn crop. It is the soil, not the calendar that will let you know when to start. It must be dry enough to work, not cold, wet or sticky.

The goal is to have planting conditions just right. Planting too early is a waste of time because if the soil is

too cold, sprouts won't grow and tubers may rot. On the other hand, waiting too long deprives the potato crop of the time necessary to mature. Though the tops thrive in long, hot days, the tubers form in cooler soil.

Many experienced gardeners have their own formulas for deciding when to plant. Some folk wisdom may not be applicable, but it is usually interesting and always contains a grain, or at least a seed potato, of truth.

THE INDUSTRIAL POTATO

A PANCAKE SYRUP SUBSTITUTE WAS AN EARLY BY-PRODUCT OF POTATOES.

In Virginia, the first weekend after Easter is the time to plant for many, despite the fact that this holiday skips around the calendar. In Michigan, some gardeners plant their potatoes in the dark of the moon in June with consistent success. In southern New England, when peonies and black locusts begin to bloom, potatoes are set out. In the Midwest, gardeners look to dandelions for advice. When they are blooming in

open areas, the soil is warm enough to plant.

One technique for creating the best possible conditions for early planting is raised beds. Well-drained raised beds with a lot of organic matter lose excess water early, usually don't need tilling and can be ready to plant much earlier than regular gardens. Raised beds are also easily covered with clear plastic for several weeks, which traps heat, warming the soil and destroying weeds, insects and diseases. Gardeners with little free time or limited mobility also swear by raised beds. Since they are not tread upon or compacted by garden equipment, raised beds need little labor once constructed. Retaining the soil with borders looks better and also defines the spaces.

Another way to get a head start on spring planting is to plant in the autumn. Common in northern areas where frost arrives early and stays late but not recommended for southern areas, it's risky and the key is accurate timing: too early and the potatoes sprout in the autumn rains; too late and the soil freezes solid. Local conditions will determine the exact timing: plant after the first cold snap but before the ground freezes.

A good method for autumn planting is to work compost or other organic matter into the soil right after harvest, then about a month later plant potatoes six inches (15 cm) deep and nine inches (23 cm) apart in eighteen-inch (46 cm) rows. Cover with six inches (15 cm) of compost and rake smooth, then add a thick layer of leaves to prevent freezing and thawing. To stimulate earliest growth, pull the mulch back in the spring on warm days to allow the soil to heat up. Whole small potatoes are the most likely to succeed under these stressful conditions.

Soaking up the sun, sweet potatoes need ninety to one hundred twenty hot, humid days to mature. Plant them after the last frost, when nighttime temperatures are above 55°F. (13°C.), and soil is at least 50°F. (10°C.).

Basic potato planting guidelines

For common potatoes, planting trenches are usually made with a hoe to a depth of eight inches (20 cm) and a width of six inches (15 cm). Two and one-half to three feet (76 to 91.5 cm) apart is standard row width, depending on your tilling methods. Some gardeners add compost to the bottom of the trench, but never fresh manure. For those in particularly hot climates or with loose, sandy soil, planting should be a little deeper.

The whole small or cut pieces of seed potatoes are firmly placed cut side down, eyes or sprouts up, in the trench, about a foot (30.5 cm) apart. Planted closer together, they produce a large number of smaller tubers. If set eighteen inches (46 cm) apart, you will find larger, but fewer potatoes when you harvest. Cover the seed potatoes with about four inches (10 cm) of soil, tamped lightly with the hoe.

For sweet potatoes, a ridged row six to twelve inches (15 to 30.5 cm) tall is made with a hoe, with three to four feet (91.5 to 122 cm) between rows. Slips are set into the soil twelve inches (30.5 cm) apart and with all of the stems buried up to the first leaves.

Hilling up

With common potatoes, new potatoes form above the seed potato, not below it, so to encourage as many potatoes to grow as possible, the practice of hilling up has evolved. Hilling up has other benefits as well. The extra soil covering prevents potatoes' being exposed to light and "greening." Hilling creates a natural irrigation ditch between rows and helps keep weeds in check.

> "BE EATING ONE POTATO, PEELING A SECOND, HAVE A THIRD IN YOUR FIST, AND YOUR EYE ON A FOURTH."
>
> *Old Irish saying*

To hill up, a hoe or rake is used to draw loose soil from between the rows when plants are six to eight inches (15 to 20 cm) tall. Plants are covered until only two to four inches (5 to 10 cm) of leaves are showing. If growing late-season varieties, repeat the hilling up two to three weeks later.

LAZY BED POTATOES

Deep mulching with an organic material such as hay or straw is an excellent method of growing common potatoes. It utilizes space and water more efficiently than traditional planting methods, encourages growth of cleaner, better-formed tubers, keeps the soil cool and evenly moist, helps prevent scab and minimizes potato bugs, keeps weed competition and weeding to a minimum, eliminates damage to tubers from cultivating, makes harvesting simple and adds humus to the soil. To create a lazy bed of potatoes, you can use raised beds or an area prepared as you would for conventional planting. It should be no

more than six feet (2 m) wide, enabling you to reach from both sides, with the length determined by your own space and planting needs. A slight mounding or slope will help if your climate is especially rainy.

To plant, simply place the seed potatoes, cut side down as usual, twelve inches (30.5 cm) apart in all directions, and twelve inches (30.5 cm) from the borders. Press seed potatoes firmly into the soil before spreading the mulch. First choices for mulch are hay, straw or shredded leaves, but anything normally used for mulch can be considered. Use caution with any mulches like sawdust, wood chips or bark, because these tie up nitrogen as they decompose. Square bales of hay are applied in six-inch-thick (15 cm) sections. Loose materials are applied twelve to eighteen inches (30.5 to 46 cm) deep, with the hotter the climate the greater the depth.

If mulch can blow away, anchor it. A bit of loose soil, wire or wooden slats will do the job. Usually mulch mats down enough to stay put. Just make sure the potatoes do not show through the mulch during the growing season, or they will green; additional mulching may be needed dur-

ing the growing season. The only other negative aspect is that in a very wet climate or with a soil with poor drainage, mulch can allow slugs or fungus diseases to thrive. The next step is harvesting. Turning back the mulch, an abundant crop is uncovered with no digging.

Another method of mulching is to plant in traditional six-inch deep (15 cm) trench rows and cover stems with organic material as they grow. Or, plant directly on a thick layer of mulch rather than bare soil. This mulch planting can utilize last year's mulch as the bottom layer, with fresh material used to cover the plot. The great aspect of this method is that there is no need for tilling or digging to prepare the potato plot.

For sweet potatoes, a shallower organic mulch, six to eight inches (15 to 20 cm) deep, is beneficial for maintaining even soil moisture and preventing weed growth. Apply it when the soil is warm but before the vines spread.

PLASTIC AND FABRIC MULCHES

No longer do southern gardeners have a corner on sweet potato production. With the advent of using sheets of black plastic for mulch, gardeners discovered that the soil was warmed and kept evenly moist enough to double sweet potato yields in northern climates.

Several different materials are available for this use. There is a porous black plastic with millions of microscopic holes allowing water, nutrients and air to penetrate. Another advancement in plastic mulches is the infrared transmitting type (IRT mulches), that combine the weed-control benefits of black plastic with the superior heat absorption of clear plastic. The porous fabric, or polyolefin, mulches also have the attributes of inhibiting weeds while allowing water, air and nutrients to penetrate. There

are different types and thicknesses of these, with some being sturdy enough for use five years or more if carefully taken up and stored each autumn. Biodegradable paper mulches are a special blend of peat moss and recycled cardboard and can be tilled into the soil at season's end.

Using any of these couldn't be simpler. Most of these materials are available in three- or four-foot-wide (91.5 or 122 cm) rolls, which neatly cover ridges two to three feet (61 to 91.5 cm) wide and six to twelve inches (15 to 30.5 cm) high. Edges are anchored by covering with soil. Cut holes every twelve inches (30.5 cm), plant sweet potato

slips, and settle back with a lemonade. In the autumn, cut off the top growth, peel back the cover, and harvest your bumper crop of sweet potatoes.

While optimal for sweet potatoes in the North, plastic or fabric mulches can benefit common potatoes, too. Most successful with raised beds, the sheets of material are placed over the soil, holes cut and potatoes planted.

Container growing

Believe you don't have room to grow potatoes? Think again! Success stories abound of abundant crops emerging from containers. An additional bonus with container

growing is the visual pleasure. The lush foliage of both common and sweet potatoes growing up and spilling over the sides of a container is as decorative as any annual yet has the benefit of a hidden treasure. Containers are also an ideal way to let children grow their own crop.

Bushel baskets, plastic trash bags and barrels and the full gamut of other containers can be used. Just be sure the container has drainage holes. For common potatoes, a minimum of eighteen inches (46 cm) deep is necessary to allow space for tubers to form. A container at least twelve inches (30.5 cm) deep and fifteen inches (38 cm) wide is enough for sweet potatoes.

For common potatoes, add six inches (15 cm) of soil-less potting mix or garden soil enriched with compost or composted manure to the container. Set seed potatoes six to eight inches (15 to 20 cm) apart, then cover them with two to four inches (5 to 10 cm) of soil. As the potatoes grow, more potting mix or soil is added, or a combination of compost, straw and soil.

Sweet potato slips are planted in containers filled with a soil-less potting mix or a light, porous soil mix, spacing six to twelve inches (15 to 30.5 cm) apart. Bush varieties are usually best, but if growing a vining variety, allow stems to trail or train on a trellis or stake for support.

Place the containers in a sunny location and keep evenly watered. Depending on the fertility of the soil used,

a light feeding during the growing season should be considered.

TIRE TOWERS

Stacking three or four old automobile tires is one unusual way of growing potatoes. Start with one tire, placed either on a paved surface or on soil. Fill the tire with six inches (15 cm) of sandy loam soil enriched with compost, composted manure or other organic soil amendment. Plant two or three seed potatoes and cover with a layer of soil. As the plants grow, successively add more tires and soil, keeping only about six inches (15 cm) of plant above the soil level. Go no higher than four tires.

Again, locate in full sun and keep well watered. When the plants yellow in the autumn, dismantle the tire tower and harvest. You should not be surprised if a bushel of potatoes turns up!

WIRE TOWERS

With this method, cut a six-foot (183 cm) length of three- or four-foot-high (91.5 or 122 cm) standard chicken

PLANTING TIMES

Area	Spring/Summer Harvest	Autumn Harvest
COASTAL SOUTH	JAN., EARLY FEB.	LATE AUG., SEPT.
LOWER SOUTH	FEB., EARLY MARCH	LATE JULY, AUG.
MIDDLE SOUTH	MAR., EARLY APRIL	LATE JUNE, JULY
UPPER SOUTH	APRIL, EARLY MAY	JUNE, EARLY JULY

YEAR-ROUND PLEASURE

Sweet potatoes makes one of the lushest vining houseplants possible. You'll need a location with bright sunlight, at least a six- or eight-inch (15 to 20 cm) pot and soil-less potting mix. A whole small sweet potato can be half buried horizontally in the soil or a sweet potato slip planted. Feed and water regularly.

wire or wire fencing and loop into a circle, fastening the ends. Space towers twelve inches (30.5 cm) apart if making more than one.

Put four inches (10 cm) of hay in the bottom and cover with two inches (5 cm) of rich garden soil. Set four seed potato pieces on the soil and cover with two more inches (5 cm) of soil. As the potato plants grow, more soil is added, with additional hay lining the perimeter of the tower and holding in the soil, until it reaches the top of the tower. To harvest, the tower is simply unfastened or pulled up.

VERTICAL GARDENING BINS

You can also build a three- or four-foot-square (91.5 or 122 cm) bin, similar to a wooden compost bin, out of two-by-six-inch (5 × 15 cm) boards for the sides and two-by-four-inch (5 × 10 cm) corner posts, attaching the side boards so there are two inches (5 cm) of space between them. Use wood screws for assembly to make disassembly easy. Put in a six-inch (15 cm) base of soil enriched with compost or composted manure and lightened with vermiculite or perlite. Set presprouted seed potatoes around the perimeter so that the sprouts grow toward the light from the two-inch (5 cm) spaces. Cover with six inches (15 cm) of soil. Repeat to the top of the container. The top layer is planted with seed potatoes over the whole area, with the sprouts aiming up, not sideways. Cover with a final layer of soil. The hardest part of this method is keeping it well watered, but the rewards are great, with a potential yield of fifty pounds (23 kg) from sixteen square feet.

SUCCESSION PLANTING

IN CLIMATES WITH A LONG GROWING SEASON, WHICH ALSO USUALLY HAVE HOT SUMMERS, COMMON POTATOES ARE BEST GROWN EARLY IN THE SPRING OR IN THE AUTUMN. THE CHART ABOVE GIVES THE RANGE OF PLANTING TIMES FOR A SPRING, SUMMER AND AN AUTUMN HARVEST.

SIX

Tuber Loving Care

PAMPERING YOUR POTATOES

otatoes are generally care-free crops compared with many vegetables, but as with any life form, a certain amount of tender loving care pays off.

Whether you use a shallow or deep mulch, no other gardening technique benefits both you and the potatoes more. As discussed in Chapter 5, a mulch minimizes the time you'll have to spend weeding, watering and controlling pests, plus it makes harvesting easier and adds nutrients to the soil.

Both common and sweet potatoes need a steady supply of water throughout the growing season but never so much that the soil is soggy. The balance between enough water and optimum drainage is critical. Water is most important as plants begin to develop tubers. Depending on the climate and variety, this is about six to ten weeks after planting.

What happens if the plants are deprived of water? The tubers grow very little and plant cells begin to mature. If this drought period is followed by an abundant supply of water, the plants react with a second growth spurt. The tubers develop odd shapes and cracks. To prevent this a consistent supply of water to a depth of eight to ten (20 to 25 cm) inches is recommended. If you can't count on rainfall and don't think mulching will offset evaporation and drainage, then the best method of watering is with a drip irrigation system. The easiest to use are the porous hose systems.

If you have prepared the soil well, the fertile potato bed should need little additional feeding during the growing season. Some gardeners add a bit of fertilizer between the plants, not on them or their roots, when hilling up young common potato plants. Most people prefer to not risk the danger of overfeeding their potatoes. There is nothing more disappointing than encouraging growth to the extent that the luxuriant green tops produce no tubers to eat. And the danger of using fresh manure on potato beds cannot be overemphasized. Feeding of the potato garden is best done in advance.

POTATO BEASTIES

Potatoes from certified disease-free stock and resistant varieties, rotated annually, not stressed from weeds, inadequate nutrients or water, and grown in a garden with thorough postseason cleanup and that encourages natural pest enemies will have a minimum of insect and disease infestations.

Not that there aren't bugbears out there: Over two hundred sixty diseases can affect potatoes. Most are never a problem in home gardens. In mass monocultures, pests are a major problem and farm-raised potatoes have had ninety-six pesticide residues detected in them. Peeling potatoes helps to lessen the effects of pesticide residues, but the best solution is growing your own using a minimum of the safest possible pest controls.

IN JUNE OF 1992, THE VICE PRESIDENT OF THE UNITED STATES, DAN QUAYLE, IN AN ATTEMPT TO PROVIDE ASSISTANCE TO A SPELLING-BEE CONTESTANT, SPELLED POTATO "POTATOE." IN HIS DEFENSE THE VEEP CITED GEORGE WASHINGTON AS USING THE SAME SPELLING.

POTATO PEST CHART

PEST	APPEARANCE	DAMAGE	CONTROL
Aphids	Less than one-eighth inch (3 mm) long, pear shaped with long antennae and two tubes projecting back from the abdomen; may be grey, black, brown, yellow, red, lavender or green; live in clusters under leaves or on growing tips; wings develop in crowded colonies; found all over North America; often associated with ants, who use and protect them; excrete a substance called honeydew, which can develop sooty mold; attack both common and sweet potatoes	Suck sap from leaves and stems, causing foliage to curl, pucker and turn yellow, then brown and die; spread viruses	Sticky yellow traps; wash off with strong water spray; insecticidal soap; rotenone; pyrethrum; sabadilla; homemade garlic or tomato leaf sprays; don't plant potatoes near roses; many natural predators, with lacewings the best
Blister Beetle, Potato Bug	One-half- to three-quarter-inch (1 to 2 cm) adults are metallic black, blue, brown or purple, with elongated bodies and necks, long legs and flexible wing covers; larvae start tiny but turn into fat grubs with heads; found all over North America but worst in East	Feed on foliage, defoliating plants of both common and sweet potatoes	Hand-pick and drop into pails of soapy water, wearing gloves as they can burn and blister skin; rotenone; sabadilla; pyrethrum; blister beetles are of benefit to garden because larvae feed on grasshopper eggs, so value judgment must be made
Colorado Potato Beetle, Potato Bug	One-quarter inch (6 mm) long; yellowish orange or light tan with ten vertical black stripes; bright yellow-orange egg clusters on undersides of leaves hatch into fat red grubs with black spots; found throughout North America, but not considered a problem in California and Nevada	Pest of common potatoes; both grubs and beetles devour leaves, leaving a lacy leaf skeleton	Resistant to many pesticides; hand-picking works on a small-scale plot—is best done by shaking plants in the morning onto a ground cloth; straw mulch; floating row covers; eaten by spined soldier bugs, lacewings and lady beetles; *Bt san diego*; rotenone; pyrethrum; homemade sprays made of eucalyptus, cedar or basil; wheat bran on leaves causes beetles to bloat and burst; toads, ladybugs and chickens are natural predators; horseradish planted at each corner of the potato patch; 'Sequoia' and 'Katahdin' show some resistance
Flea Beetles	One-eighth inch (3 mm) or less; black, brown or bronze with large hind legs; name comes from how they jump; found throughout North America	Chew holes or grooves in sweet potato leaves; cause dark, rough, deformed common potato tubers	Floating row covers; white sticky traps; parasitic nematodes; pyrethrum; rotenone; sabadilla; 'Jewell' is a tolerant variety
Cutworms	Several sizes and colors; usually one inch (2.5 cm) long with shiny heads; adults are grey or brown moths; found throughout North America	Live in soil and cut off young common potato plants at ground level at night or feed on young tubers	Put paper collars around young plants at ground level; parasitic nematodes; apply pellets of *Bt berliner-kurstake* mixed with a molasses-bran bait to soil surface a week before planting

PEST	APPEARANCE	DAMAGE	CONTROL
European Corn Borer	One-inch-long (2.5 cm) white, pink or brown caterpillars with brown spots; adults are yellowish or brown moths; eggs are masses of white clusters on undersides of leaves; found in northern and central United States and eastern Canada	Feed on foliage and stems of common potatoes	Efficient garden cleanup; *Bt berliner-kurstake*, pyrethrum; ryania; sabadilla
Leafhoppers	Look like tiny grasshoppers, one-fifth inch (5 mm) long, some with brightly colored bands on body; hold wings in a wedge shape; nymphs are wingless; found throughout North America	Both adults and nymphs suck sap from undersides of common potato leaves, causing them to become stunted, curled, stippled or browned at the tip and edges; carry viruses; even a small infestation can drastically reduce yield	Floating row covers; keep other Nightshade family members and weeds away from potatoes; garden cleanup; yellow sticky traps; insecticidal soap; pyrethrum; sabadilla; ryania
Nematodes	Knots or swellings appear on the thinner roots or they rot; both common and sweet potatoes are scarred, knobby or pitted and when cut open brown cavities reveal tiny white worms; plants may be stunted or turn yellow; occurs mainly in the South		Plant resistant varieties; rotate crops
Potato Psyllid	Greyish adults one-tenth inch (2.5 mm) long; pale green, flat nymphs	Injection of fluid into common potato tubers causes short sprouts, yellow, withered leaves	Remove and destroy infested plants; dust soil with diatomaceous earth; autumn garden cleanup
Slugs	Soft-bodied mollusks without shells; brownish, slimy; one-eighth inch (3 mm) to three inches (7.5 cm) long; leave mucus trails; found throughout North America	Eat young common potato tubers and leaves	Beer traps or food lures; sprinkle cinders, ashes or diatomaceous earth around plants and potato patch
Sweet Potato Weevil	One-half inch (15 mm) legless white grubs with dark heads; adults are one-quarter-inch (6 mm) metallic-blue heads and wings, reddish ant-like insects with thorax and legs, and long snouts; worst in the South	Grubs do most of the damage, tunneling through the roots; infested roots taste bitter; adults feed on foliage	Autumn garden cleanup, including destroying volunteer plants; certified weevil-free slips and seed potatoes; rotation; remove and destroy infested plants; destroy wild morning glory nearby; 'Regal' is a resistant variety
Symphylan, Garden Centipede	Three-eighths inch (10 mm) long with twelve sets of legs; milky white delicate adults	Feed on roots and tubers of common potatoes; stunted growth	Strong garlic tea; thorough tilling of soil; locate compost pile away from garden
Tuberworms	Larvae of grey-brown potato tuber moth; white-pink worm three-quarters inch (2 cm) long with dark head; found in about half of states, worst in South and California	Feed on outside of potato tubers, leaving superficial tunnels; webbed foliage, blotchy leaves and stems with tunnels as well; wilted plants; prevalent in hot, dry weather	Destroy affected plants and tubers; crop rotation; moist soil; organic mulch
Wireworms	One-half to one and one-half inches (1.5 to 4 cm) long; white, yellow or rust-colored larvae with pointed ends; adults are three-quarter inch (2 cm) dark click beetles	Tunnel trails in tubers; prevalent in areas previously in lawn grass	Resistant common potato varieties include 'Peru Purple Finger', 'Pink Pearl', 'Rosa', 'Siberian', and 'Austrian Crescent'; trap with potato cut in half and stuck one inch (2.5 cm) into soil, then discard in several days; predatory nematodes

DISEASES

DISEASE	APPEARANCE/DAMAGE	CONTROL
Blackleg	Common potato tubers develop black, shiny rot from the stem end; lower leaves turn yellow and upper leaves curl upward; black spots on stems; stem base rots; plants wilt and die	Sterilize knife when cutting seed potatoes and let heal over, or plant whole seed potatoes; plant certified disease-free seed potatoes; plant resistant varieties; avoid overwatering or too much nitrogen fertilizer; remove and destroy diseased plants; when harvesting, don't bruise tubers or wash
Black Rot	Sweet potato roots develop round, sunken black spots in the soil or in storage; roots taste bitter; stunted, yellowed plants; black stems	Certified disease-free slips or roots; crop rotation; remove and destroy infected plants; 'Allgold' is resistant variety
Early Blight	One-half inch (1 cm) brown spots on common potato leaves after flowering; sunken purple areas on tubers in ground or in storage with brown or black rot beneath them; worst in wet-and-dry weather	Crop rotation; autumn garden cleanup; plant certified disease-free seed potatoes; remove and destroy blighted foliage; copper fungicide; plant resistant varieties
Late Blight	Brownish black spots on leaves of common potatoes; brown streaks on stems; downy white growth on leaf undersides; brown to purple sunken spots and blotches on soggy, puffy tubers with deep lesions	Garden cleanup; destroy any volunteer potato or tomato plants; use certified disease-free seed potatoes; crop rotation; don't plant potatoes near tomatoes; copper fungicide; remove potato plants two weeks before harvesting potatoes; dry tubers well before storing in well-ventilated place; plant resistant varieties
Leaf Roll	Common potato leaves shrivel, roll up and die; tubers slowly decompose; caused by a virus	Plant certified disease-free seed potatoes; destroy diseased plants; control aphids
Potato Scab	Common potato tubers develop rough, corky spots; tubers are still edible	Plant certified disease-free seed potatoes; soil pH lower than 5.6; cool, evenly moist soil; avoid using fresh manure; crop rotation; plant resistant varieties
Stem Rot	A form of fusarium wilt affecting sweet potatoes; leaves turn yellow and fall off; stem interior is dark; roots are edible but small and rotten at stem end	Plant certified disease-free slips or roots; plant resistant varieties; destroy diseased plants
Verticillium Wilt	Appear late in season on common potatoes with lower leaves wilting and yellowing; stem interior is yellow or brown; potato eyes turn pink; malformed tubers	Destroy diseased plants; plant resistant varieties

ORGANIC PEST CONTROL

The primary consideration in controlling pests is developing and maintaining a healthy garden by means of sound cultural practices. Healthy soil is regularly enriched with organic matter and organic sources of nutrients so that there is a good level of humus, lots of microbial and earthworm activity and nutrients and moisture available slowly and steadily to plants. Planting resistant varieties, rotating crops and "solarizing" the soil are other cultural methods.

Biological controls can be nurtured or introduced into your garden as allies in the battle against plant-eating bugs. These include aphid midge, *Bacillus thuringiensis (Bt)*, convergent lady beetle, green lacewing, praying mantids, predatory mites, predatory nematodes, spined soldier bug, trichogramma wasp, whitefly parasite as well as bats, garter snakes, toads and salamanders.

In addition, there are physical means of keeping the pest populations at insignificant levels in the garden. Means range from hand-picking pests to barriers such as floating row covers, baited traps that draw insects away from your food crops and sticky traps that attract with color and that the insect physically adheres to.

Save organic chemical controls for last-ditch efforts. Whether homemade solutions of herbs and hot peppers or the pests themselves, or purchased sprays and dusts derived from plants or other natural sources, these are still toxic substances even though they are not persistent in the environment or manufactured from nonrenewable resources. Recommended organic pesticides include insecticidal soap (but not on bright, sunny days when it may burn the foliage), diatomaceous earth, agricultural sulfur, copper compounds, neem, pyrethrum, rotenone, ryania and sabadilla.

Combined with the above four aspects, the best protection against insect infestations and diseases is a regular inspection of your garden and plants. All these problems are easiest to control when first noticed. Usually minor precautions work unless the problem is allowed to reach epidemic proportions. A few beetles can be picked off by hand, a few wilted plants removed. Don't wait until your entire harvest is at risk. Before you take any action, look at the bigger picture. Thinking about possible interactions and aftereffects with the rest of your garden is as important as eliminating the specific problem at hand. *Always* begin with the least extreme solution. Often it will do the trick.

POTATO TROUBLESHOOTING

Not all garden problems are the result of insects or diseases. Sometimes the problems are from poor cultural practices. The following list describes some of the potential problems that your potatoes may have that can be remedied by simply changing some aspect of growing, harvesting or storing.

COMMON POTATO TROUBLESHOOTING

PROBLEM	POSSIBLE CAUSE	REMEDY
Hollow heart; irregular hole in the center of a common potato, often with brown discoloration; usually affects very large tubers; will rot in storage	Rapid and uneven growth; watering too much after blooming; prolonged moisture after a drought; too much fertilizer; planting too far apart, which overstimulates growth	Apply enough water in times of drought; mulch with at least four to six inches (10 to 15 cm) of hay or straw to ensure moisture retention
Green tuber; green color is from chlorophyll, which is harmless, but exposure to light increases the glycoalkaloid content of the potatoes and the two bitter-tasting toxins, solanine and chaconine. Most potatoes ordinarily contain two to nine milligrams of these substances per serving, but toxin levels can triple in only eight hours of exposure to light, with more than twenty milligrams causing alkaloid poisoning, resulting in headaches, fever and diarrhea	Exposure to sun while growing, curing or in storage	Hill up potatoes as they grow; keep storage dark; peel and cut away green parts; discard very green potatoes; do not leave potatoes in the sun to dry
Soapy texture, noticed when preparing to cook	Harvesting main crop too soon	Harvest later
Too sweet	Storage in an area that is too cold causes starches to turn to sugar	Recondition, or reverse effect, by putting potatoes in a warmer place
Net necrosis; brown netting or streaking in raw potatoes	Near-freezing temperatures kill the food-conducting cells, called phloem, which are more susceptible to temperature than the other storage cells	Harvest and store potatoes that are more mature; increase temperature in storage
Tan streaks throughout tubers	Hot, dry weather causes stress	Add organic matter to soil; water; mulch; plant drought-tolerant varieties
Potatoes turn black after cooking	Stored at temperatures above 100°F. (38°C.) or potassium deficiency	Store at cooler temperatures; add potassium source, such as greensand, to soil
Bumpy, deformed, knobby, dumbbell-shaped tubers	Early drought; high growing temperatures (over 80°F. [27°C.]); too much nitrogen in soil	Plant earlier; add organic matter to soil; water; mulch; grow corn for a season or two before planting potatoes there again
Tubers mushy or rubbery on inside	Drought causes tuber to give up moisture to leaves	Adding organic matter to soil; watering; mulching
Spindly shoots	Too warm and dark when sprouting; sprouts have suffered a freeze or have a disease	Provide cooler temperatures when sprouting; use certified disease-free seed potatoes
Small tubers	Late planting; drought; soil too alkaline; not enough phosphorus in soil; weeds; harvested too early; poor-quality or improperly stored seed potatoes; not enough sunlight during growing season; too much nitrogen in soil	Plant earlier, lower soil pH; add phosphorus to soil; harvest later; buy certified disease-free seed potatoes; grow in sunnier location; grow corn for a season or two before planting potatoes there again
Transparent spots on tubers	Tubers freeze before harvest	Harvest before freezing weather

PROBLEM	POSSIBLE CAUSE	REMEDY
No potatoes, but plants are flourishing	Too much nitrogen in soil	Do not add fresh manure or nitrogen fertilizer right before planting; grow corn for a season or two before planting potatoes there again; be sure plot is exposed to full sun
Dead tuber tissue	In warmer climates, leaving potatoes in ground after tops die in late summer	Harvest as soon as tops die back
Poor germination	Seed pieces have rotted in ground	Let seed pieces heal over; dust with sulfur to prevent rot; plant certified disease-free seed potatoes, not grocery-store potatoes; plant later or in drier weather
Yellow foliage	Plants are mature and ready for harvesting; if early in season, soil may be too dry	Mulch; water; add organic matter to soil
Hard and inedible microwave- or foil-baked potatoes	Not using a "baking" variety	Some potatoes are not good for baking, especially red-skinned varieties, which often have a higher water content; Russet types are better for baking

SWEET POTATO TROUBLESHOOTING

PROBLEM	POSSIBLE CAUSE	REMEDY
Roots rot in storage	Bruising and scarring when digging up; skins not properly cured	Carefully dig and handle gently; after digging, leave on top of dry soil for a couple of hours, then cure in a warm (70° to 80°F [21° to 27°C.]) place for two weeks
Parts still hard after cooking	Stored too cold; left in ground too long	Do not store potatoes in the refrigerator or cold root cellar; harvest before cold weather sets in; may have cork disease
Poor flavor	Drought; left in ground in cold weather; too much nitrogen in soil	Water; mulch; add organic matter to soil; harvest earlier; grow corn for a season or two before planting potatoes there again
Dark brown skin	High organic content in soil	Use less organic matter in soil; problem is cosmetic

Beetle-Resistant Varieties

Leptine is a chemical that potato beetles don't like to eat. It naturally occurs in some wild potato varieties. These are being bred with commercial varieties in the hopes of developing a potato that the potato beetle won't eat.

The Blender Solution

Perhaps they release pathogens, odors or pheromones signalling danger, but whatever the reason, gardeners have success combining insects with a cup or two of water in a blender, straining the mixture, and mixing one part insect puree with four parts water. Spray all over the plants, undersides as well as tops of leaves. Another homemade bug repellent is a tea made by pouring boiling water over one tablespoon wormwood leaves, one teaspoon garlic, two tablespoons chives, one teaspoon hot pepper, and two tablespoons mint. Let steep for several hours, strain and dilute with 4 parts water. Spray on all plant surfaces. Add a teaspoon of liquid soap to make it adhere to the leaves.

The Peripatetic Colorado Potato Beetle

First described in 1824, these black-striped orange beetles ate nightshade weeds in their native Colorado. When the gold mines were started in 1858, settlers brought potatoes. While young men went West, the beetle went East. By 1865 it had crossed the Mississippi. In four more years it was on the East Coast. During World War I it spread to the Bordeaux region of France, probably by way of American soldiers and their grub. Then it traveled throughout France, into Belgium and Germany. After many counterattacks, it managed to gain entry to England as well.

SOME BLACKLEG-RESISTANT VARIETIES OF COMMON POTATO

Katahdin • Kennebec • LaRouge • Red LaSoda • Red Norland • Red Pontiac • Superior

SOME VERTICILLIUM-RESISTANT VARIETIES OF COMMON POTATO

Alaska Red • Atlanta • Beltsville • Elba • Green Mountain • Katahdin • Ona • Pontiac • Red Dale • Rhinered • Rideau • Shoshoni

SOME SCAB-RESISTANT VARIETIES OF COMMON POTATO

Alasclear • Alaska Frostless • Anoka • Atlantic • Banana • Beltsville • Bison • Butte • Caribe • Carola • Cherokee • Chieftain • Early Ohio • Gold Nugget • Idita Red • Indian Pit • Jemseg • Kipfel • Krantz • LaRouge • Norchip • Norgold "M" • Norgold Russet • Norkata Russet • Norland • Onaway • Ontario • Purple Marker • Red Dale • Red LaSoda • Red Warba • Redsen • Rhinered • Rideau • Russet Burbank • Sebago • Siberian • Sierra • Superior • Warba

SOME BLIGHT-RESISTANT VARIETIES OF COMMON POTATO

Alaska Red • Atlantic • Bison • Brigus • Cherokee • Chieftain • Elba • Idita Red • Katahdin • Kennebec • Kipfel • Onaway • Ontario • Pink Pearl • Rhinered • Sebago

SOME STEM ROT-RESISTANT VARIETIES OF SWEET POTATO

Allgold • Centennial • Jasper • Nemagold • Southern Queen • Triumph • Yellow Strassburg

SOME WILT-RESISTANT VARIETIES OF SWEET POTATO

Beauregard • Centennial • Jewell • Sumor

SOME NEMATODE-RESISTANT VARIETIES OF POTATOES

SWEET POTATOES
Heart-O-Gold • Jasper • Jewell • Kandee • Nemagold • Nugget • Sumor

COMMON POTATOES
Beltsville • Elba

SEVEN

One Potato
Two Potato

HARVESTING AND STORING POTATOES

To carefully wriggle one's fingers into the warm, soft, welcoming earth, then gently bring forth a tender, delicate new potato is one of those pleasures of the garden that brings a sigh of contentment and a feeling of all being right with the world. For people who cherish the indulgences of the garden, such subterranean treasure hunts are reason enough to plant potatoes.

By growing the early-season varieties, you can harvest small new potatoes just eight weeks after planting. Mid- and late season varieties may not have new potatoes ready for ten weeks or so. Test for size a week or two after flowering begins. Egg or golf ball-sized tubers are large enough for an incomparable meal. If you want to have part of the crop mature, be sure to leave some potatoes with each plant, carefully putting the soil and mulch back in place.

Few people know that you can also harvest sweet potatoes when young. This is something you'll never see in stores, and they are indescribably delicious.

For common potatoes, dry yellow vines are a sign that the potatoes are fully mature.

Check one or two potatoes by rubbing the skin with your thumb. If it doesn't rub off, the tubers are ready for harvest and storing. For the potatoes to form a thickened skin, the tops have to be dead or removed. A thick skin is what allows for longer storage. As long as the vines are alive, both common and sweet potatoes continue to increase in size.

If you have to harvest before the foliage dies because of cold weather, cut the tops off a few days before potatoes are dug. Common potatoes can withstand being in the ground for a few weeks after the first frost if you have no time to harvest immediately. The tubers will be dormant but still must be kept in the dark. Don't let them actually freeze, as they will become watery and unusable. Mature sweet potatoes can withstand a light frost, which will kill the tops, but should be harvested as quickly as possible. It is better to harvest before plants are frosted.

Ideally, choose a fairly dry period for your final harvest. Digging when the soil is wet does more than just muddy your Wellingtons, it is damaging to the soil. Using a spading fork, dig a foot or more from the main stem to avoid cutting into the outly-

ing potatoes. Most of the crop will be at the same distance away, so after the first try, the rest of the digging can copy. If using the deep mulching method, simply pull back the mulch. Be sure to dig into the soil to see if any potatoes are hidden there.

Treat potatoes gently when digging and preparing for storage, as rough handling can bruise them and cause blackening problems in storage. Never drop a potato more than six inches (15 cm). Bruising also increases in cold weather.

A CHOOSING RHYME USED BY SCHOOLCHILDREN, USUALLY BY COUNTING ON OUTSTRETCHED FISTS: "ONE POTATO, TWO POTATO, THREE POTATO, FOUR. FIVE POTATO, SIX POTATO, SEVEN POTATO, MORE."

After harvesting and before storage, potatoes need to go through a curing process that thickens the skins adequately for storage. With sweet potatoes, it also converts starches to sugars, which gives them their special flavor. Never wash potatoes at any stage in this process, waiting instead until ready to prepare them.

To cure, first let newly dug potatoes dry for a couple of hours on top of the ground. For common potatoes, cure for one to two weeks in a dark, dry spot at 65° to 75°F. (18° to 24°C.). Sweet potatoes are cured in a dark, warm (80° to 90°F. [27° to 32°C.]) area with high humidity for one to two weeks. Spread tubers out while curing so they do not touch. At the end of the curing period, inspect potatoes, discarding any that show signs of injury or disease.

Early-season common potatoes do not store for long periods. They are best used in four to six weeks. During that time, store them in a dark location with temperatures between 40° and 70°F. (5° and 21°C.). Mid- and late season potatoes can be kept in a dark location for up to six months with temperatures of 35° to 40°F. (2° to 5°C.) and 85 to 90 percent humidity. Sweet potatoes will keep for up to six months when stored in a dark location at 50° to 60°F. (10° to 16°C.) and 60 to 70 percent humidity.

Avoid storing potatoes with apples or pears. The ethylene gas produced by the fruit hastens the sprouting process in potatoes. Potatoes also rot more quickly when stored with onions. If limited space does not allow you to separate these crops, good ventilation will prevent some of the ensuing problems. Air circulation is very important to successful storage, both in

THE FIRST MATURE POTATOES WERE RITUALLY EATEN BY THE ENTIRE FAMILY TO ENSURE THAT THE STORED CROP WOULD LAST.

the storage space and in the boxes or bins used.

Picky gardeners will wrap each potato in newspaper, then place them gently in

boxes. Even the most casual gardeners know to not store potatoes in deep bins, as their own weight can damage the tubers on the bottom. Porous sacks, such as burlap or paper, or wooden or open plastic crates are the best solution. Bins should be no more than eighteen inches (46 cm) deep. Holes in the sides and bottoms are helpful, as is layering with straw. Do not use plastic bags. In December, check potatoes again for signs of spoilage, discarding the rotten ones.

Do not store potatoes in a refrigerator. Cold temperatures cause common potatoes to develop an unpleasant sweetness. If this occurs unavoidably, it can be reversed by storing potatoes in the dark at 70°F. (21°C.), then returning them to the optimal storage at 35° to 45°F. (2° to 7°C.). Refrigerated storage causes sweet potatoes to darken and eventually shrivel and rot. Potatoes that freeze will become inedible, turning black, mushy and rotten.

Storage locations
A traditional root cellar, like those found in older homes, with a dirt floor and stone walls, is often the ideal spot, but storage can be created easily in modern surroundings. For instance, use a

garage or shed that does not freeze. A cellar stairwell with a door at the bottom of the steps is often the proper temperature and humidity. In a modern basement, find a corner that can be walled off from the rest of the space, insulate it against heat from the furnace and provide air exchange through a window or other ventilation system. Make sure the humidity is kept high.

A window well can be improvised into storage space. First, rodentproof it by placing hardware cloth at the bottom, then putting down a layer of straw. Add potatoes, then cover with more straw and weatherproof it with boards and a waterproof covering. Access it through the window from the basement.

Other techniques include burying an old refrigerator, sinking a drainage tile or garbage can into the ground or half-burying a storage barrel

at a 45-degree angle and covering with straw. A traditional method that doesn't require much time or money is called "the clamp" in England or a vegetable mound in the United States, with many variations. In moderate climates, choose a well-drained spot out of harsh wind. Put down a foot (30.5 cm) of straw as a base. On top of that place cured tubers in a pyramid-shaped pile. Cover with another thick layer of straw. Lay a few boards around it for protection or put a layer of soil on top. For colder climates, dig a hole one foot (30.5 cm) deep and three feet (91.5 cm) square. Line it with hardware cloth to keep out rodents. Next, line it with four inches (10 cm) of bedding, such as straw, hay or dry leaves. Place a pyramid of tubers in this space and cover with another foot (30.5 cm) of bedding. Finally, twelve inches (30.5 cm) of soil is mounded up over this. A small portion

> ## "TWO THINGS ARE TOO SERIOUS TO JOKE ABOUT: MARRIAGE AND POTATOES."
>
> *Old Irish saying*

of bedding material extends out through the peak of the mound for ventilation. An irrigation ditch may be needed to drain water away. Place boards over the top to keep animals out.

An alternative is to dig twelve-inch-deep (30.5 cm) holes, placing potatoes in each, and covering with soil, then layers of wood chips, leaves and grass clippings to two feet (61 cm) high. This will withstand temperatures down to $-20°F.$ ($-29°C.$).

In warmer climates, storage problems are different. If temperatures after harvest are still on the warm side, a cool storage spot may be hard to find. The coolest spot may be in the house, inner closets or pantries if there is no cellar.

For greater details, the definitive book for home gardeners on the subject is *Root Cellaring* by Mike and Nancy Bubel (© 1979, 1991, 2nd edition, by Storey Communications, Pownal, VT).

FREEZING POTATOES

Generally, it is not recommended to freeze potatoes for storage, although the first potato growers in the Andes had their own "freeze-drying" method. Preservation of food is extremely important in any society, and the early South American cultures were no exception. Though potatoes are good keepers compared with most vegetables and fruits, longer-term solutions still had to be developed. The worst enemy of these early farmers was frost, but they learned to harness it for their own purposes.

Making *chuno* was an early means of freeze-drying, developed before the Incas, possibly as early as two thousand years ago. The method involves spreading the tubers on the ground and leaving them to freeze overnight. During the day, groups of people stomp on them repeatedly to press out the water. Several days are needed to complete the process. By then the desiccated, lightweight tubers are ready to be stored for long duration.

Easy to transport, *chuno* was also a medium of trade. The Spanish conquerors soon found a use for it, too, buying it cheaply from the producers to feed to their native slaves

> THE USDA HAS CREATED A SUPER POTATO POWDER ABLE TO ABSORB THOUSANDS OF TIMES ITS WEIGHT IN LIQUID.

who worked the silver mines.

Today, home freezing of potatoes is usually done only after cooking. Even then potatoes in soups and stews freeze poorly, tending to disintegrate when reheated. Mashed and baked stuffed potatoes and patties work best. To freeze, cool quickly in the refrigerator, place in freezer containers or use freezer wrap, and store at 0°F. (−18°C.) for no more than a month. For frozen french fries, prepare by baking pieces at 450°F. (230°C.) until they just turn brown, then chilling quickly in the refrigerator. Wrap and freeze for no more than two months. Another way to precook them is to blanch them quickly in hot oil. To reheat either type,

bake at 450°F. (232°C.) until golden brown or deep-fry at 390°F. (199°C.) until crisp.

To save time when making hash browns or other recipes calling for shredded potatoes, potatoes can be grated and frozen. To prepare, use a food processor or hand grater. Ten pounds (4.5 kg) of potatoes will fill about sixteen one-quart (0.95 l) freezer bags. Wash and peel potatoes. Keep in cold water until all are prepared. Grate the potatoes, put into a colander or strainer and drain. Steam for three minutes, being careful to not overcook. Return potatoes to the colander and dip in ice water to cool. Drain well and form into patties about two-by-four inches (5 × 10 cm) and one-half inch (1 cm)

SOME OF THE BEST KEEPING POTATOES

ALASKA FROSTLESS
BISON
BLUE VICTOR
CARIBE
CARIBOU
COWHORN
EARLY OHIO
INDIAN PIT
KATAHDIN
LEMHI RUSSET
NOOKSACK
NORGOLD "M"
RED NORLAND
RED WARBA
SENECA HORN
SIBERIAN
YELLOW FINN
YUKON GOLD

thick. Wrap in wax paper and freeze on a baking sheet for a few hours. Remove and pack in freezer wrap or one-quart (0.95 l) freezer bags. To use, defrost in the microwave, remove wax paper and bake on a baking sheet at 325°F. (163°C.) until tender and golden. Broil for a crisper pattie.

EIGHT

This Spud's For You

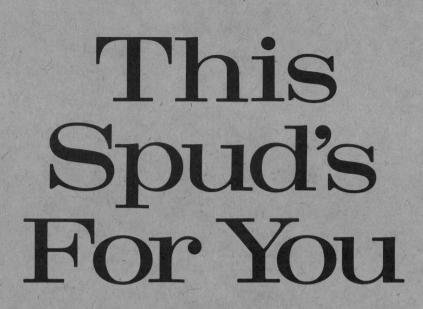

POTATO PORTFOLIO

Life is a mystery. Why else would department stores be filled with thousands of different styles and colors of clothing year after year, which obviously get purchased, yet 80 percent of the potatoes consumed in the United States derive from just six of over five thousand varieties available? At the supermarket, the choice among potatoes is usually between large, elliptical baking potatoes and small, round red- or tan-skinned ones, all with white flesh. At very innovative food purveyors, the selection may increase to include one yellow-fleshed type.

Where are the pale yellow-fleshed 'Austrian Crescent' fingerlings begging simply to be boiled and eaten with salt and pepper and perhaps a dollop of yogurt? What about 'La Rota', favored by French chefs for firm yellow flesh and tantalizing flavor? Where is 'Caribe', that makes the lightest, fluffiest mashed potatoes ever? Or 'Butte' with its extra 20 percent of protein? Or 'German Butterball', that has been described as having "taste beyond your imagination"? And who could not fall in love with 'Alaska Sweetheart' with its red skin and red flesh? Or have fun making blue french fries or lavender vichyssoise from 'All Blue'?

America, we are being shortchanged! Arise and find out just how great our favorite comfort food can be. Sustenance taken to a higher order is ours for the growing. As described in this book, more than enough common and sweet potatoes for your delectation can be easily grown without harmful pesticides with only a minimum of effort and space.

The most difficult part is in choosing which varieties to grow. Even though the five thousand named cultivars are not all in commerce, selecting from among the several hundred that are available is no mean feat. Still, we should be grateful.

To be dependent upon only a handful of varieties is only slightly less foolhardy than the Irish dependence on one variety in the early 1800s. Having a diversity of varieties ensures a genetic pool that provides a wide range of levels of starch, protein and vitamins, plus resistance to insects and viral, bacterial and fungal diseases necessary for future breeding work.

The more unusual potato varieties becoming available again today from commercial growers were carefully saved and preserved from year to year for us by institutions and private growers and collectors who valued their special spuds enough to keep them alive for future generations. Many "lost" varieties continue to turn up in all corners of the world, as people are informed of the value of their family traditions.

Keeping heirloom varieties going is hard work. In addition to commercial growers, many dedicated potato lovers put in lots of labor to ensure the continuity of their favorite plants. Since a variety must be replanted, harvested and stored anew each year, this job is not simply accumulating a museum collection. It is a task that allows no break. The horticultural heritage found in heirloom plants, potatoes as well as others, is as important to our history as artifacts of art, literature or music.

Historical farms and villages are valuable repositories of botanical antiques. Dedicated individuals such as the members of Seed Savers Exchange as well as institutions such as the Interregional Potato Introduction Station in Wisconsin or the International Potato Center in Lima, Peru, and mail-order sources like Ronniger's, Seeds Blum, or Fred's Plant Farm maintain an invaluable mother lode of genetic material.

This work, combined with that of the plant breeders who utilize these varieties plus the wild species in their development of more nutritious, better tasting and more pest-resistant cultivars, has established a well-rooted potato renaissance.

> **"THERE IS NO SPECIES OF HUMAN FOOD THAT CAN BE CONSUMED IN A GREATER VARIETY OF MODES THAN THE POTATO."**
>
> *Sir John Sinclair, 1828*

In choosing the potato varieties for growing in your garden, you'll want to take into account not only your climate, site and soil but also what aspect will be most satisfying to you. Do you prefer your potatoes baked? Then by all means grow some of the Russet types. If tiny new, red-skinned potatoes are your idea of heaven, then look to the early-maturing varieties. For potato-salad lovers, the fingerlings are ideal. To have potatoes all winter long, choose at least one variety that excels in storage. If concerned with nutrition, choose the varieties with extrahigh levels of protein or vitamins A or C. These are just a few of the criteria to consider. Some gardeners focus on pest resistance or production. The choice is yours.

One important criterion in choosing common potatoes is the maturation period. Potatoes are grouped into three types. Early-season potatoes mature quickly, sometimes in as few as fifty-five or sixty days and continuing for up to ninety or so days. They are planted in early spring and are usually very hardy. Most do not store well. Midseason potatoes are planted a few weeks after the early potatoes and harvested in midsummer, or in about eighty or more days. Some types store well.

Late-season potatoes are planted at the same time as midseason types but harvested after the vines die down in the autumn, or in ninety days or more. They are excellent for winter storage.

Let the planting begin!

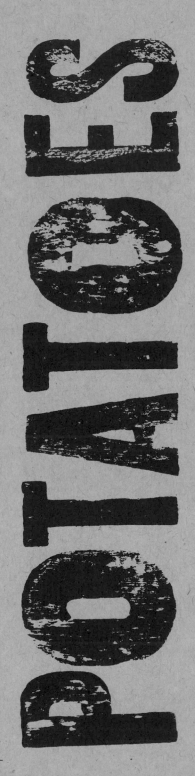

POTATOES

COMMON POTATO PORTFOLIO

ACADIA RUSSET

midseason; Canadian origin with attractive blooms; elongated oval tubers; smooth, russeted skin; vigorous growth; good for boiling and baking

ALASCLEAR

midseason; white skin and flesh; 'Ontario' is a parent; scab resistant; good eating quality

ALASKA FROSTLESS

midseason; flat oval, small to medium tubers with very white flesh, tan skin; produces tubers below seed piece; plants hardy to 27°F. (−3°C.)

ALASKA RED

early to midseason; hardy; developed in Alaska; red skin with snow white flesh; blight and wilt resistant

ALASKA SWEETHEART

midseason; red skin and flesh; unique and pretty

ALASKA 114

midseason; white potato; delicate; smooth skin; use in soups or stews

ALL BLUE

midseason; deep blue or purplish skin with blue flesh; blue flowers; good yields of medium tubers; excellent flavor; to keep color do not overcook

ALL RED

Red flesh; light producer; rare

ANNA CHEEKA'S OZETTE OR OZETTE

late season; fingerling; historic potato thought to have originated in Peru and traded in 1700s by Spanish explorer to Makah-Ozette tribe; grown in Northwest coastal temperate areas; prolific two- to eight-inch-long (5 to 20 cm), round tubers with thin skin, yellow flesh, and many eyes; tasty and prolific

ANOKA

early season; very early with white flesh and smooth tan skin; scab resistant; medium size; from Minnesota

ASPARAGUS

late season; long yellow fingerling; good flavor; firm texture; good yields

ATLANTIC

midseason; oval to round with white flesh; mealy, dry type for boiling and baking; ranks third in acreage in United States; popular in Maine for high yields and appearance; resistance to late blight and scab; good for northern gardens

AUGSBURG GOLD

midseason; golden skin and flesh; large, oblong shape; buttery flavor

AUSTRALIAN CRAWLER

late season; tall plants; very productive; medium tubers with deep-set eyes; flavorful; old-fashioned look

AUSTRIAN CRESCENT

late season; crescent-shaped fingerling; light yellow flesh; smooth tan skin; up to ten inches (25 cm) long; prolific; good for salads, boiled, and steamed; superb flavor

BAKE KING

midseason; oblong shape; mealy texture; good for baking; will not develop hollow heart

BANANA

late season; fingerling; long and slender with yellow flesh; scab resistant; good for salads

BELTSVILLE

midseason; round, crisp tubers; resistant to golden nematode, verticillium wilt and scab

BINTJE

late season; medium size; yellow-brown skin and yellow flesh; high-yielding; flavorful; good disease resistance; most widely grown yellow variety; originated in Holland in 1911; good keeper; grows anywhere; yellow Finnish type

BISON

early maturing; red skin, white to pale yellow flesh; shallow eyes; uniform size; good all-round potato; fries, bakes and boils well; resistant to late blight and scab

BLACK MAN'S TOES

late season; long, round, somewhat crescent-shaped dark purple tubers with white flesh; unusual and interesting

BLACK RUSSIAN

midseason; prolific; dark skin; medium; from Cornell University

WHEN YOU BUY POTATOES AT THE GROCERY, THE NAME USUALLY GIVEN, SUCH AS IDAHO, MAINE AND SO FORTH, REFERS TO THE LOCALE OF PRODUCTION, NOT THE VARIETY.

POTATOES ARE USED TO
SOOTHE SUNBURNS OR
FROSTBITE IN THE
SOUTHERN UNITED
STATES.

BLISS TRIUMPH
early season; light red skin,
white flesh; old variety from
North and Canada

BLOSSOM
midseason; smooth with red
skin and flesh; tubular shape;
opinions vary on productivity;
produces large, petunia-like
white and pink flowers; to
retain color, do not overcook

BLUE MAC
late season; increasingly
popular Canadian variety;
white flesh, blue-purple skin;
vigorous, three-foot
(91.5 cm) plants; prolific
yields of medium to large
potatoes; good for baking,
frying and boiling

BLUE VICTOR
late season; one of the first
blue varieties; long popular;
superior yields; hardy; an
excellent keeper

BRIGUS
midseason; creamy yellow
flesh; shallow eyes; uniform
round shape; heavy yields;
late-blight resistant

BUTTE
late season; noted for having
20 percent higher protein
content than most potatoes
and high vitamin C content;
large, uniform size; Idaho
Russet type; high yields; good
flavor and texture; keeps well;
scab resistant

CANDY STRIPE
midseason; white skin with
red stripes; white flesh;
flavorful; good producer;
disease resistant

CARIBE
early maturing; blue-purple
skin; snow white flesh;
excellent yields; uniform
tubers; good boiled, steamed
or mashed; resistant to scab
and storage rot

SKIPPING RHYME:
"POTATOES, TOMATOES,
CORN AND BEANS . . ."

CARIBOU
midseason; Canadian bred;
tan skin with pink-red
blotches and light yellow
flesh; medium tubers; good
productivity

CAROLA OR CAROLE
mid- to late season; smooth,
deep yellow skin and flesh;
good producer and keeper;
scab resistant; survives
drought well; from Germany

CENTENNIAL RUSSET
midseason; favored in Rocky
Mountains; brown skin with
white flesh; uniform size;
vigorous growth; good winter
keeper; baking

CHARLOTTE
extra-early season; golden
yellow skin and flesh; good
producer; medium
oblong shape

CHEROKEE
late season; thin, smooth,
light tan skin with white
flesh; medium size; good for
boiling; stores well with high
flavor retention; resistant to
scab and blight; grows in clay
and muck soils

CHERRIES JUBILEE

late season; smooth cherry pink skin with delicate pale pink flesh; small, rounded tubers; good for new potatoes; late harvest stores well

CHERRY RED

midseason; bright red skin with white flesh; good for new potatoes; heavy yields

CHIEFTAIN

mid- to late season; best seller in Canada; smooth red skin with white flesh; high yields; uniform medium size; good quality; resistant to scab and late blight

CHIPPEWA

early season; smooth, light tan skin with white flesh; shallow eyes; round to oval medium tubers; good yield; flavorful; boils and mashes well; good keeper; resists mosaic but susceptible to scab; good in peat and muck soils; popular in East and Midwest

COASTAL RUSSET

midseason; oblong, Russet-type; white flesh; good yields; tolerates scab; good baker; poor boiled

COWHORN

late season; old variety, possibly from New Hampshire; horn shape; light purple skin and off-white flesh; good for baking with mealy, firm flesh

CRYSTAL

hybrid with white skin and flesh; said to be whitest of all potatoes; reliable, all-purpose variety; disease resistant

DARK RED NORLAND

midseason; burgundy skin with white flesh; keeps well; slightly later than Red Norland; good salad potato

DAZOC

early season; red potato with deep eyes; from North Dakota; flavorful; stores well; good for baking and hash browns

DELTA GOLD

midseason; pale tan skin with yellow flesh; uniform medium to large tubers; from Maine

DENALI

midseason; from Alaska; high yields in dry conditions; baking potato with dry, mealy flesh; also mashes well

DESIREE

midseason; pink-red skin with yellow flesh; prolific; good all-round cooking potato popular in Europe; disease resistant

DONNA

midseason; red skin with yellow flesh; good yields; does not store well; good for baking; sweet, moist texture

EARLY ANNE

early season; white skin and flesh; from Pennsylvania Amish with Irish Cobbler parentage

EARLY GEM

very early season; reliable and uniform; from North Dakota

EARLY OHIO

early season; tan skin with white flesh; flavorful; good for frying; very firm; keeps well; an early 1900s heirloom popular in Midwest

EARLY ROSE

early to midseason; light pink skin with white flesh sometimes streaked with pink; vigorous growth; large yields; long tubers

EIDE RUSSET

midseason; round shape; good productivity; Minnesota origins

ELBA

early season; Katahdin-type with good appearance and yields; large white potato; average vigor; resistant to early and late blights, wilt and golden nematode; from Cornell University

CRAMOSA

early season; large, round tubers; good yields; developed in Canada for northern climates; resistant to hollow heart

HOT POTATO

A TERM USED TO DESCRIBE A TOUCHY TOPIC, ONE WITH A LOT OF DISSENT OR NO SOLUTION. SOMEONE IS SAID TO BE HOLDING A REAL HOT POTATO. ALSO CAN MEAN A BEAUTIFUL WOMAN.

EXPLORER

early to midseason; variety grown from true seed; boiling or baking

FENTON BLUE

late season; heirloom variety from Maine; purple skin and blue flesh; uniform in shape; very prolific

FRONTIER

improved version of Butte; 20 percent more protein than most potatoes; uniform oblong shape; white flesh; from University of Idaho

GARNET CHILE

late season; heirloom; parent to many potato varieties; rosy or red skin; round eyes; thick skin; keeps well

GERMAN BUTTERBALL

late season; outstanding taste; smooth yellow skin and flesh; large round oblong tubers

GERMAN YELLOW

late season; fingerling; golden skin and rich yellow flesh; medium to large; excellent flavor and texture; prolific; good keeper

GLACIER

midseason; deep blue skin with blue-white starburst flesh; shallow eyes; round oblong shape; from Alaska

"JUST GIVE ME MY POTATO, ANY KIND OF POTATO, AND I'M HAPPY."

Dolly Parton, The New York Times, *April 29, 1992*

GOLD NUGGET

midseason; only Russet type with yellow flesh; good producer with medium to large tubers; buttery flavor

GREEN MOUNTAIN

late season; tan skin with white flesh; popular since 1885; excellent producer in a variety of soils; keeps well and retains flavor for a long time; mealy texture; poor disease resistance

HAIDA

late season; fingerling; grown by West Coast Indians for over 100 years; large white tubers with deep eyes; very prolific

HAIG

early to midseason; flaky skin with white flesh

HARMONY BEAUTY

midseason; pale yellow skin with cream flesh; old type from Maine

> PUT SMALL NEW POTATOES IN A DRY BISCUIT TIN. COVER WITH DRY SAND, SEAL THE TIN WITH CARE AND BURY IN THE GARDEN. MARK YOUR SPOT WELL AND DIG THEM UP FOR CHRISTMAS. THEY WILL TASTE AS GOOD AS SUMMER NEW POTATOES.
>
> *In Praise of the Potato*
> Lindsey Bareham

HILITE

early season; Russet type; high yield of No. 1 bakers; vigorous and disease resistant

HOMESTEAD HYBRID

late season; hybrid grown from true seed; vigorous; uniform, rapid growth; large tubers

HUCKLEBERRY

midseason; beet-maroon skin with white marbled red flesh; medium tubers; good producer; vigorous

HUDSON

late season; round oblong tubers; buff skin with white flesh; does well in dry weather

HUMBOLDT RED

midseason; light reddish skin; large, long, flat shape; flavorful; good keeper; originated in mountain areas of northern California

IDITA RED

midseason; red-gold skin; scab and blight resistant; hardy plants

IMPROVED PERUVIAN PURPLE

late season; developed from Peruvian Purple; more intense color; more vigorous plants

INDIAN PIT

late season; highly waxy; small to medium; tan skin with white flesh; eyes splashed with pink; flavorful; good for long-cooked stews and campfire cooking

IRENE

late season; pink-red skin with yellow flesh; smooth, round uniform tubers; excellent keeper; disease resistant; from the Netherlands

IRISH COBBLER

early season; popular old favorite introduced in 1870s; cream skin; oblong, flat shape with shallow eyes; mealy texture good for mashing; consistent yields; grows everywhere; susceptible to scab; resistant to mosaic

ISLE OF NORTH GERMANY

late season; brought over by German settlers in 1800s; golden skin with yellow flesh; flavorful; produces many medium to large tubers

MEAT-AND-POTATOES MAN

JACKSON WHITE

yellow-white skin with numerous deep eyes; medium to large tubers with irregular shape; originally from Maine; dry mealy flesh with good flavor

JEMSEG

very early season; tan skin with white flesh; grows in heat and drought

JULY

very early season; rose skin with cream flesh; from the Pennsylvania Dutch and Amish

KATAHDIN

late season; popular in eastern United States since 1932; round and white; good yields; adaptable to many soils and climates; stores well; resists mosaic and blight; susceptible to scab; good flavor; popular for mashing, baking and all-purpose use

KENNEBEC

midseason; famous Maine potato; large elliptical shape; light tan skin with shallow eyes and white flesh; consistent grower; good keeper; excellent for frying, hash browns and all-purpose use; plant sunburns easily; resistant to blight and mosaic; stores moderately well; heavy yields; widely available

KIPFEL

late season; fingerling; crescent shape; medium to large; yellow potato with shallow eyes; large yields; resistant to scab and blight; stays firm after cooking

KRANTZ

midseason; buff skin with white flesh; uniform oblong shape; medium to high yields; stores well; good baker; resistant to late blight and scab; susceptible to early blight; short dormancy so does not store long

LADY FINGERS

mid- to late season; fingerling; brown skin with yellow flesh; small to medium size; for steaming, boiling or frying; excellent flavor; brought over by early German settlers

LA ROTE OR LAROTA

late season; fingerling; buff yellow skin and flesh; French gourmet potato; firm flesh and unique flavor

LAROUGE

midseason; red skin with white flesh; oblong shape; gaining popularity as a market variety; scab resistant

LEMHI RUSSET

late season; commercial variety widely grown in West; netted skin with white flesh; baking potato with excellent flavor and keeping quality

LEVITT'S PINK

midseason; rose-pink skin with pink-red flesh; medium-long round tubers; light producer

MANDEL

late season; fingerling; crescent shape; yellow flesh; excellent flavor and texture for salads, baking and roasting; prolific; drought and disease resistant

A SCIENTIFIC ACADEMY IN THE UKRAINE HAS CLAIMED THAT POTATOES ARE A POTENTIAL ENERGY SOURCE FOR RUNNING ELECTRIC GENERATORS.

MAYFAIR

creamy buff skin with white flesh; shallow eyes; high yields of medium-large tubers; for baking, boiling and frying

McNEILLY

sets all season; red skin and light yellow flesh; excellent keeper

MICHIGOLD

midseason; round; rough skin with yellow flesh; good producer; moderately good keeper; very flavorful; from Michigan

---

BY THE LATE NINETEENTH CENTURY, THE REVEREND RICHARD SEWALL BLAMED THE POTATO FOR LEADING HOUSEWIVES TO RUIN BECAUSE IT WAS SO SIMPLE AND QUICK TO PREPARE.

MRS. MOEHERLE'S YELLOW

midseason; yellow skin and flesh; good flavor; medium size

NETTED GEM

late season; same as Russet Burbank; good baker; excellent keeper

NOOKSACK

late season; Russet type for coastal and wet regions; heavy yields; large baking potatoes with dry flesh; stores well

NORCHIP

commercial variety used for potato chips; for southern states; smooth skin with white flesh; good flavor

NORGOLD "M"

early season; for southern states; withstands dry soil; Norgold Russet flavor; tough skin for baking

NORGOLD RUSSET

early season; heavy netted Russet-type skin with shallow eyes and white flesh; consistent grower; scab resistant; excellent baking and boiling potato; from North Dakota; does not store well; matures before danger of frost damage in northern areas; also good for southern areas

NORKOTA RUSSET OR RUSSET NORKOTA

early season; smooth skin with white flesh; uniform, dependable yields; good storage; good variety for limited-space gardeners; scab resistant; for baking, frying or boiling; from North Dakota; ranks third in U.S. production

---

THE GAME OF SPUD IS A FORM OF DODGE BALL, WITH SCORE KEPT BY "SPUDS," OR POINTS AGAINST A PERSON.

NORLAND

very early season; smooth red skin with white flesh; medium oblong tubers with shallow eyes; widely adapted favorite of home gardeners; good yields; excellent for boiling and baking; can discolor after cooking; resistant to scab; widely available

NORWEGIAN

late season; fingerling; rose to pink skin and yellow flesh; medium long, slender tuber; sweet flavor; good for salads and broasting; produces and keeps well

NOSEBAG OR FRENCH FINGERLING

late season; purple-pink skin with yellow flesh; medium tubers

ONAWAY

early season; buff skin with white flesh; round with shallow eyes; good yields; scab and blight resistant; good winter keeper

ONTARIO

midseason; tissue-thin, smooth, tan skin with white flesh; good yields; fine cooking quality; resistant to scab and early and late blight

PERU PURPLE FINGER

purple skin and flesh; cook with skin on; makes excellent potato salad

PINK CRESCENT

good flavor; stores extremely well; recommended for Northwest

PINK PEACH

midseason; rose-pink skin with creamy yellow flesh; medium tubers

PINK PEARL

late season; pink skin with white flesh; oblong tubers; large plants; good for boiling, steaming, frying or roasting; resistant to wart and blight; good keeper

PINTO

midseason; skin yellow with splashes of red; creamy flesh; good producer

PURPLE CHIEF

midseason; deep purple skin with white flesh; prolific; medium to large oblong tubers; excellent keeper; from Canada

PURPLE MARKER

midseason; purple skin and flesh; disease and scab resistant

PURPLE PERUVIAN

late season; fingerling; purple skin and flesh; medium size with many eyes; hardy plant; mealy flesh; very good keeper

RED CLOUD

mid- to late season; red skin; medium to large tubers with shallow eyes; heavy yielder; good keeper; use boiled, baked or stewed

RED DALE

early season; red skin with white flesh; large, round, flat tubers; prolific; good keeper; resistant to scab and wilt

PEANUT

late season; fingerling; brown netted skin with yellow flesh; peanut shape; from Sweden; long popular in Alaska; flavorful; prolific; hardy; good keeper

MR. POTATO HEAD®

A CLASSIC CHILDREN'S TOY WITH A LENGTHY POPULARITY AND ENDLESS POTATO PERMUTATIONS. TODAY'S VERSION INCLUDES A PLASTIC SPUD.

RED DUTCH

early to midseason; red skin with yellow flesh; prolific; medium, mealy tubers

RED ERIK

early season; red skin with shallow eyes; heavy yields; moderate resistance to scab and late blight; susceptible to verticillium wilt; tolerates wet soil; good steamed, boiled or baked

RED GOLD

early to midseason; light red skin with yellow flesh; high yields; medium round tubers; disease resistant; use for boiling, steaming and frying

RED LaSODA

midseason; smooth red skin with deep eyes and white flesh; adaptable; popular in South; tolerates high temperatures; good producer; use for boiling and salads; not good for baking; moderate keeper; widely grown commercially; susceptible to disease

RED NORLAND

early season; smooth red skin with white flesh; good yields of medium to large tubers; stores well

RED PONTIAC

mid- to late season; thin, dark red skin with shallow eyes and white flesh; round shape; heat tolerant; will grow in heavy soil; high yields; good keeper; for mashed potatoes and boiling, not baking; widely available

RED WARBA

early season; old standard; smooth red skin with white flesh; oval shape

REDSEN

midseason; red skin with white flesh; prolific; medium tubers; good flavor; grows in wet coastal climates

RHINERED

early season; popular in Midwest; red skin with deep eyes and white flesh; round to oblong, medium to large tubers; good yields; better baked than boiled; resistant to scab, blight, wilt and silver scurf; short dormancy and limited storage

RIDEAU

midseason; bright red skin with snow white flesh; medium to large size; heavy yields; resistant to scab and verticillium wilt; good for mashing

> THE MOTTO ON THE IDAHO LICENSE PLATE SINCE 1948 HAS BEEN "FAMOUS POTATOES."

ROSA

tan-pink skin with white flesh; small size; high yields; excellent flavor

ROSE FINN APPLE

late season; fingerling; rose-buff skin with deep yellow flesh; firm waxy texture; good flavor; prolific; medium tubers

ROTE ERSTLING ROSE

early season; red skin with yellow flesh; oblong shape; disease resistant

RUBY CRESCENT

late season; fingerling; rose skin with yellow flesh; fine flavor; good keeper; use for steaming or baking

RURAL NEW YORKER

late season; old-time Northeast variety; russeted white skin and flesh; all-purpose cooking; stores well

RUSSET BURBANK

late season; same as Idaho Baker, Idaho Russet or Netted Gem; russet skin with shallow eyes; for baking, frying or boiling; needs consistent moisture supply; originated from Luther Burbank's early plant breeding; most widely grown in United States; good keeper; scab resistant

RUSSET CENTENNIAL

late season; brown skin with white flesh; long tubers; bake or boil

RUSSIAN BANANA

late season; fingerling; popular in Canada with people of Baltic origins; medium size; yellow salad type; excellent disease resistance

> MASHED POTATO IS THE GENTILE'S CHICKEN NOODLE SOUP. IT'S NATURE'S TRANQUILIZER, I TAKE IT INSTEAD OF VALIUM.
>
> *Love After Lunch*
> Andrew Payne

SANGRE

early season; red skin; prolific; small tubers; for boiling; good keeper

SEBAGO

late season; popular in Southeast; strong plants; white skin; round to oblong tubers; all-around cooking potato; resistant to scab and blights; heavy yields

SENECA HORN

late season; grown by Iroquois Indians in upper New York State; purple skin with white flesh; vigorous plants

> "AN ATTACHMENT À LA PLATO FOR A BASHFUL YOUNG POTATO, OR A NOT-TOO-FRENCH FRENCH BEAN!"
>
> Bunthorne in *Patience*
> Sir William Gilbert

SEQUOIA

midseason; tan skin with white flesh; large tubers; good resistance to insects and sunburn

SHAW #7

midseason; smooth purple skin with shallow eyes and purple flesh

SHEPODY

mid- to late season; Russet type; buff skin with white flesh; grown for french fry production; also good for boiling or baking; uniform high yields; susceptible to scab

ELVIS PRESLEY IS SAID TO HAVE EATEN MASHED POTATOES EVERY NIGHT FOR THE LAST YEAR OF HIS LIFE.

SIBERIAN

late season; yellow to white skin with purple blotches and deep eyes; firm and flavorful; oblong shape; scab resistant; good keeper

SIERRA

early season; Russet type; uniform tubers; resistant to scab and hollow heart; excellent keeper; from Canada

SNOWFLAKE

early season; white skin and flesh with shallow eyes; hardy; good keeper

STEUBEN

early to midseason; white flesh; high yields; flavorful

SUPERIOR

early season; smooth tan skin with shallow eyes and white flesh; large, uniform shape; widely grown along East Coast and in the South; tolerates varied soils but not severe drought; does not grey or discolor with cooking; good keeper; scab resistant; susceptible to late blight

TRIUMPH, OR RED BLISS

early season; pale pink skin; good baker; susceptible to blight; developed 1878

BUBBLE AND SQUEAK IS A TRADITIONAL ENGLISH DISH MADE OF MASHED POTATOES, COOKED CABBAGE AND ONIONS. THE NAME MAY COME FROM THE SOUND OF THE MIXTURE COOKING IN THE PAN OR THE SOUNDS FROM ONE'S STOMACH AFTER EATING IT.

URGENTA

midseason; pink-orange skin with yellow flesh; long tubers; resistant to wart; drought tolerant; good for new potatoes, mashing, boiling or salads; popular in Europe

VIKING PURPLE

midseason; unique with true purple skin with deep red splashes; good keeper

VIKING RED

midseason; red skin with white flesh; uniform large round tubers; for baking, boiling or mashing; good keeper; space closely; good drought tolerance; harvest before they become oversized

WARBA OR WARBA PINK EYE

early season; golden skin with reddish pink splashes around eyes; uniform oval tubers; scab resistant; for steaming, boiling or frying; excellent keeper

WASECA

midseason; red skin with yellow flesh; medium round tuber; good yields

WHITE BANANA

late season; fingerling; prolific; large tubers; white flesh

WHITE COBBLER

early season; popular variety; flavorful; mealy texture; good for baking or all-purpose use; poor storage

WHITE ROSE

midseason; large elliptical tubers; smooth white skin with many deep-set eyes and white flesh; does not store well

YELLOW FINN

midseason; yellow-tan skin with waxy yellow flesh; excellent keeper; versatile for all kinds of cooking, especially soups; popular in Europe

YELLOW FIR

similar to Lady Finger; blush pink skin; odd protrusions on crescent-shaped tubers

> I APPRECIATE THE POTATO ONLY AS A PROTECTION AGAINST FAMINE, EXCEPT FOR THAT I KNOW OF NOTHING MORE EMINENTLY TASTELESS.
>
> *La Physiologie de Gout*, 1825
> Brillat-Savarin

YELLOW ROSE

midseason; pinkish skin with yellow flesh; for steaming or salads; good yields

YUKON GOLD

early season; smooth, thin yellow skin with yellow flesh; good flavor; for boiling or baking; uniform yields; excellent keeper; plants have a tendency to spread

Sweet Potato Portfolio

All Gold

semibush type; high yields; orange skin and moist pink-orange flesh; cans and stores well; susceptible to nematodes; resistant to viral disease, internal cork and stem rot; good for Midwest; very high in vitamin A

Beauregard

high yields; short season; red-orange skin with orange flesh; little cracking; from Louisiana; wilt resistant; susceptible to nematodes

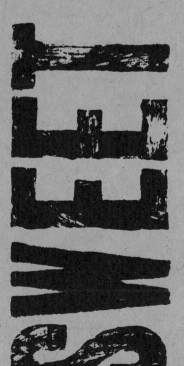

Bermuda Pink

vining; long season; pink skin with cream flesh; ribbed roots

Burgundy

deep purple flesh; color does not fade with cooking

Caromex

variety specially adapted for growing in parts of New Mexico

Carver

long vines; large potatoes; red skin with deep orange moist flesh; unique flavor; early; developed at Tuskegee University; named after George Washington Carver

> ONE OF THE GREATEST LUXURIES . . . IN DINING IS TO BE ABLE TO COMMAND PLENTY OF GOOD VEGETABLES, WELL SERVED UP. EXCELLENT POTATOES, SMOKING HOT, AND ACCOMPANIED BY MELTED BUTTER OF THE FIRST QUALITY, WOULD ALONE STAMP MERIT ON ANY DINNER: BUT THEY ARE AS RARE ON STATE OCCASIONS, SO SERVED, AS IF THEY WERE OF THE COST OF PEARLS.
>
> *The Original*, 1835
> Thomas Walker

Centennial

most popular variety in United States; early, short season; fine-grained, sweet, tender, moist-flesh type; copper-colored skin with deep orange flesh; vigorous vines to twenty feet (6 m); resistant to fusarium wilt; tolerant of potato wireworm and flea beetles; good keeper; very high in vitamin A

Copperskin

copper-colored skin with orange flesh; good producer; potatoes concentrated under plant

EXCEL

vining; resistant to seven insects, eliminating need for pesticides; high yields; similar to Southern Delite; orange skin and flesh

FRAZIER WHITE

long season; good size and shape; white skin and flesh; heirloom variety

GARNET RED

semibush; pink skin with pale orange flesh; round shape; heavy producer

GEORGIA JET

high yielding; early maturing; dark red skin with moist orange flesh; uniform size tubers; recommended for both northern and southern gardens

GEORGIA RED

vining; red stems and green leaves; red skin with yellow-orange flesh; large, round tubers; cracks badly; good producer

GOLDRUSH

bush type; pale foliage; light yellow skin and flesh; high in vitamin A

HEART-O-GOLD

white skin and bright orange flesh; high quality; can be eaten before curing; bruises easily, making storage difficult; good for home garden; resistant to root knot nematode

JASPER

resistant to root knot nematode

JERSEY ORANGE

orange, dry-fleshed variety

JERSEY YELLOW

long season; similar to Jewell but with red skin and yellow flesh; easy to grow; good for South

JETS

early maturing; good choice for northern growers, even Canada; dark red skin and moist orange flesh

THE POTATOE . . . IS A VERY USEFUL ROOT, BEING EITHER BOIL'D OR ROASTED IN HOT EMBERS; AND AFTER IT IS BOILED AND BEATEN IN A MORTAR, IT IS USED TO THICKEN SAUCES FOR MAKING OF RICH PUDDINGS.

The Country Housewife and Lady's Director, 1736 Richard Bradley

SURE YOU CAN JUGGLE A FEW BEFORE YOU COOK THEM, BUT AMERICAN INDUSTRY AND INGENUITY HAS FOUND OTHER WAYS TO PLAY WITH TUBERS.

JEWELL (ALSO CALLED JEWEL OR GOLDEN JEWELL)

early, productive in diverse climates and soils; uniform; fine-textured, deep orange flesh; contains 50 percent more vitamin A than other sweet potatoes; good for baking, canning, storage; resistant to wilt, root knot nematode, and flea beetles; lead commercial variety; represents 75 percent of commercial crop

KANDEE

resistant to root knot nematode

NANCY HALL OR YELLOW YAM

vining; old favorite variety from 1930s; cream skin and pale yellow flesh; juicy, waxy and sweet; resistant to soft rot

NEMAGOLD

resistant to root knot nematode

NEW JEWELL

an improved Centennial variety; red skin with deep orange flesh; soft-textured baker

NUGGET

red skin with dry orange flesh

OKLAHOMA RED

long tubers; red skin with orange flesh

OLD KENTUCKY

vining; produces tubers away from center of plant; white skin with cream-colored flesh; sweet; excellent keeper; high yields

PELICAN PROCESSED

white flesh

POPE

very long vines; developed for growing in flood-prone areas

PORTO RICO (ALSO CALLED VINELESS PORTO RICO, BUNCH PORTO RICO, AND PUERTO RICO)

bush type recommended for limited space, including containers and greenhouses; copper-colored skin with deep orange-red flesh; good for baking; very moist and sweet

PURPLE

vining; deep purple flesh; keeps color after cooking; heirloom variety; moist and sweet; productive

RED CARVER

variation of Carver but with redder skin; popular in Georgia, where red-skinned varieties are favored

POTATO TRAP

A SLANG FOR MOUTH.

RED JEWEL
semibush; red-orange skin and flesh; moist; bakes quickly with a soft texture; easy to grow; developed in New Jersey; old variety newly reintroduced

RED YAM
vining; red skin with orange flesh; large tubers

REGAL
new type from USDA Vegetable Research Lab in Charleston, SC; high yields; purplish red skin; good flavor for baking; disease resistant

SOUTHERN DELITE
variety developed for natural insect resistance; good flavor

SOUTHERN QUEEN
vining; produces tubers away from center; white skin; tubers may be long and skinny

SUMOR
semibush; true white variety; developed by USDA Vegetable Research Lab in Charleston, SC; combines heat tolerance with starchy texture of white potatoes; substitute for white potatoes in hot climates; resistant to wilt, root knot nematodes and wireworms; high yields concentrated under plant; very productive; stores for up to a year, sweetening slightly; if cooked right after harvest, tastes like a white potato; less vitamin A than yellow sweet potatoes, but high in vitamin C; bake, mash, cream, fry or use in salads

TRAVIS
short vines; orange skin and flesh; very productive; concentrates tubers under plant; resistant to soil rot

COOK POTATOES IN STOCK OR MILK INSTEAD OF WATER. STOCK YIELDS A RICHER FLAVOR, WHILE MILK GIVES A MILDER, SWEETER FLAVOR.

HALF OF A RAW POTATO IS TRADITIONAL FOR REDUCING THE SWELLING AND DISCOLORATION OF A BLACK EYE, POSSIBLY BY DRAWING OUT FLUIDS. IT ALSO WILL HELP RELIEVE PUFFINESS.

VARDAMAN
bush type; developed by Mississippi Agricultural and Forestry Experimental Station; purple and dark green leaves; very ornamental; orange skin and deep red-orange flesh; prolific; good keeper

WHITE CRYSTAL
cream-colored skin and flesh

WHITE DELITE
vining; pink skin with white flesh; mildly sweet; good yields

WHITE TRIUMPH OR WHITE BUNCH
vining; white skin and flesh

WHITE YAM
semibush; white skin and flesh; dry; good yields; tubers clustered at center; grows well in North

WHITESTAR
white flesh

NINE

DO THE MASHED POTATO

EATING POTATOES

When life is hard, we long for what is comforting and familiar. Ask a dozen people what they want to eat when they're having a bad day, and many will say potatoes. Are potatoes consoling because they are the original nursery food, mashed with milk and butter, creamy smooth and soothing to both palate and psyche? Or, is it that most Americans grew up in a time of home cooking that generally featured some form of potatoes on the dinner plate each evening, next to the ubiquitous serving of meat? Do we relate them to our mother, who was usually the one cooking those potatoes for us? For many, potatoes are also the food of social times in teenage years, in the form of the crisp and fatty french fry, soaked in ketchup, and eaten by hand while gazing into the eyes of our first significant other or endlessly talking to our best friend about that other.

Why wouldn't we associate potatoes with stability and nurturing? Easy to prepare and digest, filling and cheap, they are always there. They are the generic food in the brown wrapper, bland, boring and white. Right? Hardly.

The rainbow colors of potatoes puts the Crayola box to shame. Making the cover of *Gourmet* in 1990, potatoes are, well, hot. Newly available varieties in many shapes, sizes, textures, flavors and colors give us a culinary palate without precedent in the history of this venerable vegetable. Witness, too, that the nutritional value of the potato is not only better than what you may have thought, but is actually being improved.

NUTRITIONAL DYNAMITE
The biggest hindrance to potato consumption in the past thirty years or so has been that they are living down a reputation that is undeserved. Despite the facts, the public perceives potatoes as fattening, and dieters often give up potatoes with cake and cookies. The culprit is not the potato but rather what we put on top or how we cook it. The truth is that the potato is fat-free unless smothered with calorie-laden toppings. Because the many varieties of potatoes available to home gardeners are flavorful enough for consumption without the usual additions, potatoes are rightfully finding their way back onto plates.

Besides their exceptional flavors, potatoes offer a stellar nutritional package. A medium-sized, five-ounce (142 g) common potato has about 110 calories and a five-ounce (142 g) sweet potato 160 calories. The common potato has the edge with slightly higher amounts of protein, phosphorus, potassium and niacin, while the sweet potato wins out with calcium and most spectacularly with almost 70 percent of the recommended daily vitamin A requirement. Both provide other minerals and vitamins, plus significant amounts of vitamin C.

A criterion for foods based on the ratio of nitrogen absorption by the body for maintenance and growth is called the assessed biological value. The most biologically complete of foods is the egg with a near-perfect value of 96. The rating for the common potato is 73, actually beating out the vaunted soybean by one point.

"PRAY FOR PEACE AND GRACE AND SPIRITUAL FOOD, FOR WISDOM AND GUIDANCE, FOR THESE ARE GOOD. BUT DON'T FORGET THE POTATOES."

John Tyler Pettee
Prayer and Potatoes

Long before vitamins were understood, people knew that potatoes were a good scurvy preventative. What about the vitamin C content of potatoes? Doesn't heat destroy vitamin C? Do we have to eat potatoes raw? How much is retained after cooking? According to potato specialists, over 80 percent of the vitamin C survives in a typical baked potato. In its skin, a common potato provides almost a third of the recommended daily allowance, while a sweet potato offers almost 50 percent of the U.S. RDA (U.S. Recommended Daily Allowance). A fresh potato will have more vitamin C than one long in storage, which is another reason to grow your own.

One variety of common potato known for its high vitamin C content is 'Butte', with 58 percent more than other common potatoes. White sweet potatoes, like 'White Delite' or 'Sumor', are even better, containing more vitamin C than most tomatoes.

And what about potassium? Almost 800 milligrams come with the average common potato, more than a banana with its 450 milligrams; and 340 milligrams come with a sweet potato. Potassium aids in the utilization of proteins and retention of nitrogen and is getting credit for disease prevention lately. Strokes are said to be averted with a high intake of potassium, or the amount equal to one average potato. A study has also shown that vegetarians have lower blood pressure, also due to high amounts of potassium in their diets. They probably eat a lot of potatoes.

The complex carbohydrates in potatoes supply us with a greater percentage of our carbohydrate requirements than any other food source. Nutritionists tells us that up to 60 percent of the body's total food intake should be in the form of complex carbohydrates, which is a mixture of starches and fibers that lower blood fat, lessening the chances of arteriosclerosis, preventing cancer and improving digestion. The dietary fiber in potatoes also absorbs water, which can help you feel more satisfied and less hungry after eating.

A quest for improving on what is already pretty good seems to be the nature of man, and such is the case with potatoes. Potatoes with higher than average protein and vitamin levels are already available, and breeding work continues. Recent research

indicates that potatoes with deep-set eyes seem to be more nutritious, so the quest over the centuries for smooth potatoes may have actually reduced food value.

VERSATILITY IN COOKING

Baked, mashed, chipped, fried, roasted, boiled, hash browns, scalloped, stuffed, dehydrated flakes, precooked frozen variations, shoestring and novelty shaped, Americans eat up to one hundred twenty pounds (54.5 kg) of common potatoes each year and Europeans about twice that much. Although only about five pounds (2.3 kg) of sweet potatoes are eaten each year, these may be baked or boiled, used in casseroles or soups or made into delectable pies and other desserts.

Packed with nutrition, low in calories, available year-round. How amazing that something with those attributes not only tastes good but also is among the most versatile of foods. If the kitchen were deprived of the potato, nearly every meal would be shortchanged. Potatoes appear in recipes of almost every nationality.

No doubt, we eat potatoes in more forms than we realize. Besides the basic white potato used as a side dish in the form of mashed or baked

> **THE MASHED PULP OF ROASTED POTATOES WAS USED AS A CURE FOR THRUSH IN HORSES.**

potatoes, about half the potatoes we eat are in snack foods and other processed forms. Potatoes are hidden in many soups, stews and casserole dishes and are an important ingredient in commercially prepared foods, mostly as starches and thickeners. Potatoes are the base for many commercially available sweet desserts, usually completely disguised.

The evolution of some of our favorite potato foods is well grounded in myth at this point. For instance, that Colonial champion of the good life, Thomas Jefferson, brought the concept of fried potatoes back from France after serving as ambassador there in the 1780s, although they didn't really catch on until the twentieth century when the soldiers returned from the two world wars. They may be called french-fried potatoes, french frieds, or french fries in the United States, chips in Great Britain, or *pomme frites* in France. By whatever name, Americans consume about 5 billion pounds (2.3 million kg) of them annually. Almost all french fries are made from Russet Burbank potatoes, even though Vermonters vouch for those made from Green Mountain potatoes. Curiously, about 90 percent of the french fries consumed in Japan are processed by Americans. French fries are even being made with sweet potatoes these days. Blanching slightly before frying helps keep them crisp.

The potato chip is a truly American invention. In the late 1800s, George Crum, the chef at the Moon's Lake House in Saratoga Springs,

> **"A FINE ROMANCE WITH NO KISSES, A FINE ROMANCE, MY FRIEND, THIS IS. WE SHOULD BE LIKE A COUPLE OF HOT TOMATOES, BUT YOU'RE AS COLD AS YESTERDAY'S MASHED POTATOES."**
>
> *"A Fine Romance"*
> *Lyrics by Dorothy Fields;*
> *Music by Jerome Kern, 1936*

NY, had a customer who kept complaining that the fried potatoes were too thick. The beleaguered chef finally sliced them paper thin, and the "Saratoga chips" became a house specialty. The rest, as they say, is history.

Potato chips are the favored snack of Americans, with numbers crunching at about 3 billion dollars each year, and are eaten around the world as well, flavored according to local tastes, including with curry in India and paprika in Eastern Europe. In Britain, they

are known as crisps. Most commercial chips are 'Katahdin' or 'Norchip' and cut about one-twentieth-inch (0.1 cm) thick by spinning drums of knife blades.

Several producers are making sweet potato chips. You can make your own with less fat. Simply slice them very thin, toss with a tiny bit of canola oil, spread them out on a baking sheet, and bake in a preheated 450°F. (232°C.) oven until crisp.

Kurt Vonnegut's claim of plastic wrap being the greatest invention of the twentieth century may be disputed by those who rely on the consequential contribution of food technology to the modern-day need for immediate gratification: instant mashed potatoes. Many people don't like their potatoes without lumps, and Rebecca Rupp, in *Blue Corn & Square Tomatoes*, asserts that the best use of dehydrated potatoes is as snowflakes in Christmas movies. Brands that include the peel (thus avoiding the 20 percent nutritional loss from peeling) and have a minimum of additives do fulfill a need for the tired, weary and ravenous. Besides forever changing army KP duty, dehydrated potatoes led the way for all manner of processed potatoes to come into our kitchens, including the vast array of frozen potato forms and packages of microwavable mashed potatoes in the dairy section at the grocery.

HOME COOKING

Some people may think that preparing potatoes means little more than boiling water, and, indeed, they don't require any elaborate preparation to be exquisite, what with the range of flavors and textures available. There are some techniques, however, that make the best better.

Whether store bought or home-grown, select the proper variety for your recipe. Many potato varieties can be

> **A DIET THAT CONSISTS PREDOMINANTLY OF RICE LEADS TO THE USE OF OPIUM, JUST AS A DIET WHICH CONSISTS PREDOMINANTLY OF POTATOES LEADS TO THE USE OF LIQUOR."**
>
> *Friedrich Nietzsche*

used for a number of purposes, but some will not bake well, while others should never be boiled.

Among common potatoes, the baking, or Russet type, is the one that is mealy and dry, usually oblong, with brown, rough skin and prominent eyes. Boilers have moist, firm, waxy flesh; they are usually round, with pale, smooth, thin beige or red skin. Fingerling potatoes are also good for boiling but are small, thin and fingerlike, usually with waxy yellow flesh. The elliptical long white potatoes have slightly yellow, smooth skin with barely discernible eyes. These as well as many others are considered all-purpose potatoes.

When indecisive as to the type of potato you have, use this test: Make a solution of two parts water to one part salt. Add the potato. A waxy boiling potato floats, while a mealy one sinks.

With sweet potatoes, there are the moist-fleshed varieties that are creamy, dense, rich and very sweet, and the ones with a drier quality. The sweet ones, sometimes erroneously called yams, convert more of their starch to sugar during cooking. Although the sweeter types are higher in calories, the drier types are usually cooked with butter or cream, more than offsetting the difference. Southerners much prefer the moister types for eating, using the dry ones for animal feed. White sweet potatoes are less sweet, less "yammy" and smooth in texture. Sweet potato breeder Phil Dukes has reported that his family couldn't tell the difference between common potatoes and the white 'Sumor'.

Select potatoes that are firm and smooth. Avoid or discard potatoes that have wrinkled skin, cut surfaces, soft dark areas or green skin. If you are cooking the potatoes whole, select uniform sizes so they will be ready at the same time. Gently scrub the potatoes to clean, using a soft vegetable brush to get residual soil from recesses and eyes. Cooking whole, with the

> **POTATOES THAT CAN TRULY HEAL WOUNDS HAVE BEEN DEVELOPED BY INTRODUCING A GENE INTO THEM THAT KILLS BACTERIA.**

peel, is the best way to retain nutrients while cooking. If you must peel, keep it as thin as possible. To prevent peeled potatoes from turning dark before cooking, put them into a bowl of cold water; when ready to use, drain and dry with a towel.

When boiling potatoes, you do not need to cover them with water. An inch or so of water in the pan is sufficient, with a tight lid on the pan. Some experts suggest

substituting a pinch of sugar for salt to retain more vitamin C. An old Cajun superstition had it that potato water would poison a dog, but the truth of the matter is that it is excellent for adding to stock or using in breads.

Do your potato pancakes turn grey? A cold-water soak will prevent this, as will a little hot milk to the batter after all of the ingredients are mixed. Or, substitute sweet potatoes.

The heavy-handed practice of oversweetening the dishes made from sweet potatoes is coming to an end. Even traditional cooks realize that the flavor of sweet potatoes can stand on its own. Baked like common potatoes, sweet potatoes are sublime. If sweeteners are still desired, use honey, molasses or fruit juices, rather than refined sugar. Cooking them with apples is a special taste combination.

The tips of the sweet potato vine are eaten as greens in some parts of the world, including Asia and Africa. Considered a fine midsummer substitute for

> TO CURE A TOOTHACHE, CARRY A POTATO IN A POCKET ON THE SAME SIDE AS THE BAD TOOTH, WHICH WILL BE HEALED WHEN THE POTATO IS DRIED.

spinach, they wilt quickly and should be eaten right away. Up to four inches (10 cm) of stem can be harvested safely from a plant, up to three times. A schedule of harvesting at forty-five, sixty and seventy-five days after

planting is reasonable. Nutritionally, these greens are an excellent source of vitamins, iron and calcium.

Boiled or steamed new potatoes are the potato lover's equivalent of spring's first morel mushrooms. Plan on four to eight potatoes per serving. Gently scrub but do not peel. Cook until tender, drain, then return to the pan and shake them over low heat for a minute. Traditionally served with a little fresh parsley and butter, try substituting a bit of extra-virgin olive oil and fresh dill, fennel or garlic chives.

Roasting new potatoes with rosemary or sage and a drizzle of olive oil is one of the simplest ways to prepare potatoes, yielding a slightly crisp brown morsel with a melting center. Cut in half or quarter, arrange on a baking sheet and bake uncovered at 400°F. (204°C.) for about thirty minutes, turning them every ten minutes.

In baking whole large potatoes, temperatures are tolerated ranging from 325° to 450°F. (163° to 232°C.), with time varying accordingly. Use potatoes that weigh at least six ounces (170 g). Pierce the skin with a fork in a few places. For a soft skin, wrap in aluminum foil or rub the skin with a bit

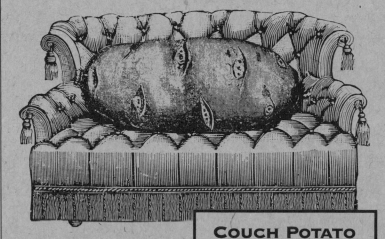

of oil before baking. Low-calorie toppings include non-fat yogurt or low-fat cottage cheese with scallions, chives, dill or other fresh herbs. Or, try caraway seeds, tiny pieces of red peppers, sesame seeds, sautéed mushrooms, onions, bell peppers or chopped green or ripe olives.

Mashed potatoes are very personal, with some people preferring to cook them in water, others favoring milk. For the smoothest mashed potatoes, heat the milk that is added when mashing. For extrafluffy potatoes, leave the pan on low heat while mashing. Keep stirring as the excess water evaporates. Many cooks swear by potato ricers, while others use an electric mixer or a traditional hand masher that leaves the requisite lumps.

A low-calorie version of

COUCH POTATO

A DEROGATORY NICKNAME GIVEN TO THE SNACK-MUNCHING, TV-WATCHING SLOUCHES WHO ARE RESPONSIBLE FOR THOSE UNBELIEVABLY HIGH NATIONAL AVERAGE NUMBER OF HOURS AMERICANS ARE SAID TO SIT BEFORE THE BOOB TUBE.

french fries is achieved with baking. Prepare the raw potatoes as usual, but instead of the deep-fat method, arrange the pieces on a baking sheet that has been coated with a vegetable oil such as canola. Sprinkle a little more vegetable oil over them and bake in a preheated 450°F. (232°C.) oven, turning frequently, for thirty to forty minutes, or until crispy and golden. Both common and sweet potatoes can be prepared this way.

Recipes

POTATO SOUFFLÉ

1 teaspoon unsalted butter or vegetable oil, preferably canola
½ cup freshly grated Parmesan cheese
1½ pounds boiling potatoes
3 fresh sage leaves
One 3-inch sprig fresh rosemary
1 cup low-fat ricotta cheese
1 cup skim milk
½ teaspoon crushed fennel seed
½ teaspoon salt
4 large egg whites
Pinch of salt

Preheat oven to 375°F. (191°C.). Butter or oil a 6-cup soufflé dish. Sprinkle 2 tablespoons of Parmesan cheese into the dish, turning it to coat all surfaces.

Wash and peel potatoes, cutting into 1-inch pieces. Combine potatoes, sage and rosemary in a large saucepan and just cover with water. Bring to a boil over medium-high heat, then lower heat and simmer for 15 minutes, or until potatoes are very soft. Drain and discard herbs.

Set the pan of potatoes back over very low heat and shake until the potatoes dry. Mash potatoes with a potato masher or ricer. Beat in ricotta cheese, milk, the remaining Parmesan cheese, fennel seed and salt.

Put egg whites into a large mixing bowl. Add salt and beat until peaks stand up straight when beater is removed. With a spatula, fold one-third of the egg whites into the potatoes, then carefully add the remainder. Spoon batter into the prepared dish. Bake for 1 hour. Serve immediately.

Makes 4 to 6 servings

A Savory Pie of Potatoes and Chard

Crust:
1½ cups grated raw white all-purpose potato
1 cup grated raw sweet potato
½ cup thinly sliced green onions
1 large egg, beaten
1 tablespoon whole-wheat flour
1 tablespoon minced fresh rosemary or thyme
1 tablespoon vegetable oil, preferably canola

Filling:
1 tablespoon vegetable oil, preferably canola
½ cup chopped onion
1 large garlic clove, minced
1 tablespoon minced fresh rosemary or thyme
4 cups torn Swiss chard leaves, with stems removed and thinly sliced
2 large eggs
1 cup skim milk
1½ cups grated Monterey Jack cheese with jalapeño peppers
1 tablespoon whole-wheat flour

Preheat oven to 350°F. (177°C.) and lightly coat a 10-inch pie pan with vegetable oil. Put the grated common and sweet potatoes in a colander or strainer. Set aside for 15 minutes, then squeeze out excess water with your hands. In a large bowl, combine green onion, beaten egg, flour and rosemary or thyme, then stir in the potatoes. Pour the batter into the prepared pie pan, smoothing it out and up the sides, patting firmly. Bake for 40 minutes, brushing lightly halfway through with the vegetable oil. Let cool slightly.

While the crust is baking, prepare the filling. Heat oil in a large nonstick skillet with a lid over medium heat. Add onion, garlic, rosemary or thyme and chard stems. Stirring occasionally, cook about 5 minutes, or until onion is soft and translucent. Add chard leaves and 2 tablespoons water. Cover and cook for 3 to 5 minutes, or until chard is wilted. Remove from heat and take off lid. In a bowl, combine eggs and milk, beating well. Toss cheese with flour and sprinkle half over the baked crust. Spoon on the chard mixture, then sprinkle with the remaining cheese. Pour the egg-milk mixture over all. Bake for 40 minutes.

Makes 6 servings

PASTEL POTATO SALAD

2 pounds small new blue- and/or pink-fleshed potatoes
¼ cup dry rosé wine
⅓ cup extra-virgin olive oil
3 tablespoons fresh lemon juice or white wine vinegar
2 teaspoons Dijon-style mustard
¼ cup thinly sliced green onions or shallots
⅓ cup minced fresh parsley
1 tablespoon minced fresh summer savory, rosemary and/or chervil
Salt and freshly ground black pepper to taste

In a saucepan, cook potatoes in boiling salted water for 20 minutes, or until tender. Do not overcook. Drain, peel potatoes if desired and cut into ¼-inch-thick slices. Put the slices in a bowl and sprinkle with the wine. In a small bowl, combine oil, lemon juice or vinegar, mustard, green onions or shallots, parsley, other herb or herbs and salt and pepper, blending well. Toss dressing with potatoes. Serve warm or chilled.

Makes 4 to 6 servings

Sweet Potato—Nut Pie

1 unbaked 9-inch piecrust shell
2 cups boiled and mashed sweet potato
4 tablespoons (½ stick) unsalted butter, at room temperature
½ cup honey
2 large eggs
1 cup milk
2 tablespoons cream sherry
½ teaspoon ground cinnamon
½ teaspoon ground cardamom
½ teaspoon ground cloves
1 cup pecans, chopped

Preheat oven to 400°F. (204°C.). In a large bowl beat together remaining ingredients except nuts. When well blended, stir in pecans. Pour into the pie shell. Bake for 15 minutes, then reduce heat to 300°F. (149°C.) and bake for 45 minutes or until filling is firm.

SWEET POTATO PATTIES

1½ pounds sweet potatoes, cut into pieces and boiled
2 tablespoons virgin or extra-virgin olive oil
½ teaspoon salt
Dash of pepper and nutmeg
¼ cup hot skim milk
½ cup pecans, chopped
½ cup pecans, ground
Butter

Drain sweet potatoes and mash with a fork, ricer or electric mixer. Add oil, salt, pepper, nutmeg and milk, beating until light and fluffy. Stir in chopped pecans and shape into 8 flat round patties. Dip both sides into ground pecans to coat. Place on a lightly oiled baking sheet and dot with butter. Bake in a preheated 450°F. (235°C.) oven for 20 minutes. Serve with a mushroom gravy.

Makes 4 servings

POTATO CURRY

4 tablespoons sesame oil
2 teaspoons ground cinnamon
2 teaspoons ground coriander seed
1 teaspoon ground cumin seed
½ teaspoon ground turmeric
2 garlic cloves, minced
1 small fresh jalapeño pepper, minced
1 teaspoon minced fresh ginger
2 medium-size onions, chopped
1 medium-size green pepper, cored, seeded and diced
½ cup unsweetened dried coconut
1½ pounds potatoes, cut into 1-inch chunks
1½ cups fresh tomato peeled, seeded and chopped
1 cup fresh or frozen green peas
¼ cup minced fresh coriander (cilantro)

Heat 2 tablespoons of oil in a large nonstick skillet over medium heat and add cinnamon, coriander, cumin, turmeric, garlic, jalapeño and ginger. Sauté, stirring occasionally, for 2 minutes. Add onions, peppers and coconut, and cook, continuing to stir, until onions are translucent, about 5 minutes.

Meanwhile, heat the remaining 2 tablespoons of oil in another large nonstick skillet over medium heat and sauté potatoes until tender and golden, or about 10 minutes. Combine potatoes with the onion mixture, tomatoes and peas and simmer for 10 minutes. Serve garnished with minced cilantro and side dishes of cucumber *raita* and chutneys.

Makes 4 servings

POTATO GNOCCHI

1 pound all-purpose potatoes
Pinch of nutmeg
Salt and pepper to taste
About ½ cup all-purpose flour
1 large egg
1 teaspoon virgin or extra-virgin olive oil
2 tablespoons minced fresh herbs such as parsley, thyme, basil, chives
and/or marjoram

Without peeling, boil potatoes in salted water until tender. Drain, cool, peel, and mash. Season with nutmeg, salt and pepper. Place potatoes on a floured work surface. Make a well in the middle and add ¼ cup flour, egg, oil and herbs. Using your fingers, quickly incorporate the ingredients together, adding more flour as you work until a soft, firm dough is achieved. Cover with a dry towel and let rest for 20 minutes. Bring a large pan of water to a boil. Roll the mixture into a long strand ½ inch thick. Cut off pieces 1 inch long and pinch ends. In small batches, drop the gnocchi into boiling water, removing when they rise to the surface, or about 5 minutes. Remove with a slotted spoon and place in an ovenproof dish in a warm oven. Serve with butter and grated Parmesan or a tomato, pesto or other savory sauce. Gnocchi may also be sautéed at this point.

Makes 4 servings

Baked Sweet Potatoes and Onions

1 pound sweet potatoes, cut into thin slices
1 pound sweet onions, cut into paper-thin slices
Salt and freshly ground black pepper
1 tablespoon minced fresh parsley
1 tablespoon minced fresh sage or thyme
2 cups pineapple or orange juice
1 tablespoon unsalted butter

Preheat oven to 350°F. (177°C.). Lightly oil a 9- or 10-inch gratin dish. Place alternate layers of sweet potato and onion slices in the dish, sprinkling each layer with salt and pepper to taste, parsley and sage or thyme. Pour juice over the top. Dot the top with butter. Cover with a piece of aluminum foil. Bake for 1 hour. Remove foil and continue baking, basting every 10 minutes, until vegetables are tender, or about another 30 minutes.

Makes 4 to 6 servings

WEISENBERGER MILLS NUTTY SWEET POTATO BREAD

3 cups self-rising flour
1 package active dry yeast
½ teaspoon nutmeg
1 teaspoon cinnamon
½ cup skim milk
¼ cup vegetable oil, preferably canola
½ cup granulated sugar
1 large egg
1 cup cooked, mashed sweet potatoes
½ cup chopped pecans

Preheat oven to 375°F. (191°C.). Lightly oil or grease a 1½-quart loaf casserole dish. In a large bowl, stir together 1 cup flour, yeast, nutmeg and cinnamon. In a small saucepan, heat milk, oil and sugar until warm (110°F. [43°C.]). Pour liquid ingredients into the flour-yeast mixture, stirring to blend. Beat in egg until smooth, or about 2 minutes with an electric mixer. Stir in sweet potatoes, nuts and remaining flour. Pour into the prepared casserole. Cover with wax paper or plastic wrap and refrigerate overnight or up to 24 hours. Remove and let rise in a warm (80 to 85°F. [27° to 29°C.]) place until doubled, or about 1 hour. Bake for 40 to 45 minutes. Serve immediately from the casserole.

Makes 1 loaf

POTATO STARCH

Potato starch was first used in the 1880s as a sizing for cotton cloth. Today, potato starch has many food and nonfood uses. In Germany, the Netherlands and Poland, extracting starch from potatoes is an important industry. First, the potatoes are cleaned in machines. Then they are disintegrated in raspers and hammer mills. The pulp is separated from the fiber in centrifugal sieves, which leaves the starch held in suspension in the liquid. It must be separated, then dried. To make potato flour, sliced potatoes are simply dried, ground and sieved.

As a food, potato starch is used as a thickener in processed food, especially puddings, instant soups, sauces and gravies. A lot of candy production and ice cream products also make use of potato starch.

Nonfood uses of potato starch include use in paper making, glues, medicines, fabrics and as a lubricant in heavy industry. New materials that should prove to be biodegradable or water-soluble are manufactured with potato starches. They are intended to replace the polystyrene "peanuts" that now clutter our lives and landfills or maybe become garbage bags. Disposable diapers contain potato starch, as do many cosmetics. It is also used in some water purification systems.

Sources

SOURCES OF WHITE AND SWEET POTATOES

Burgess Seed and Plant
Company
905 Four Seasons Road
Bloomington, IL 61701
5 common potatoes

W. Atlee Burpee Company
300 Park Avenue
Warminster, PA 18991-0001
5 common potatoes and 4
sweet potatoes

Country Heritage Nurseries
P.O. Box 536
Hartford, MI 49057
6 common potatoes

Early's Farm & Garden
Centre
P.O. Box 3024
2615 Lorne Avenue South
Saskatoon, Saskatchewan
Canada S7K 3S9
9 common potatoes

Farmer Seed and Nursery
1706 Morrissey Drive
Bloomington, IL 61704
4 common potatoes

Henry Field's Seed & Nursery
Company
Shenandoah, IA 51602
10 common potatoes and 5
sweet potatoes

Fisher's Garden Store
P.O. Box 236
Belgrade, MT 59714
6 common potatoes

Fred's Plant Farm
P.O. Box 707
Route 1, Dresden Road
Dresden, TN 38225
14 sweet potatoes

Garden City Seeds
1324 Red Crow Road
Victor, MT 59875-9713
14 common potatoes

Good Seed Company
Star Route, Box 73A
Oroville, WA 98844
Catalogue $1.00
19 common potatoes

Gurney Seed and Nursery
Yankton, SD 57079
11 common potatoes and 5
sweet potatoes

Hastings
P.O. Box 115535
Atlanta, GA 30310-8535
4 sweet potatoes and 2
common potatoes

Johnny's Selected Seeds
Foss Hill Road
Albion, ME 04910
6 common potatoes

Jung Seeds & Nursery
335 South High Street
Randolph, WI 53957-0001
7 common potatoes and 4
sweet potatoes

Orol Ledden & Sons
P.O. Box 7
Sewell, NJ 05873
7 common potatoes

Earl May Seed and Nursery
Shenandoah, IA 51603
6 common potatoes and 4
sweet potatoes

Mellinger's
2310 West South Range Road
North Lima, OH 44452-9731
7 sweet potatoes

The Meyer Seed Company
600 South Caroline Street
Baltimore, MD 21231
6 common potatoes and 5
sweet potatoes

Miller Nurseries
West Lake Road
Canandaigua, NY 14424
3 sweet potatoes

Moose Tubers
52 Mayflower Hill Drive
Waterville, ME 01901
34 common potatoes

Nichols Garden Nursery
1190 North Pacific Highway
Albany, OR 97321
3 common potatoes

Park Seed Company
Cokesbury Road
Greenwood, SC 29647-0001
1 common potato as seed, 2
as spud buds, 2 as eyes and 4
sweet potatoes

Peace Seeds
2385 S.E. Thompson Street
Corvallis, OR 97333
Seed list $1.00; catalogue and
research journal $5.00
5 common potatoes

Piedmont Plant Company
P.O. Box 424
807 N. Washington Street
Albany, GA 31703
3 common potatoes as spud
buds and 1 sweet potato

Pinetree Garden Seeds
Route 100
New Gloucester, ME 04260
15 common potatoes

Porter & Son, Seedsmen
P.O. Box 104
Stephenville, TX 76401-0104
3 sweet potatoes

Ronninger's Seed Potatoes
Star Route
Moyie Springs, ID 83845
Catalogue $2.00
188 common potatoes

Seeds Blum
Idaho City Stage
Boise, ID 83706
Catalogue $3.00
16 common potatoes

Shepherd's Garden Seeds
6116 Highway 9
Felton, CA 95018
4 common potatoes

Shumway
P.O. Box 1
Graniteville, SC 29829
3 common potatoes and 5
sweet potatoes

South Carolina Foundation
Seeds
Cherry Road
Clemson University
Clemson, SC 29634-9952
Sumor sweet potatoes

Steele Plant Company
Gleason, TN 38229
Catalogue $.50
10 sweet potatoes

Territorial Seed Company
P.O. Box 157
Cottage Grove, OR 97424
4 common potatoes

Tillinghast Seed Company
P.O. Box 738
623 Morris Street
La Conner, WA 98257
6 common potatoes

Vermont Bean Seed Company
Garden Lane
Fair Haven, VT 05743
4 sweet potatoes

Wetsel Seed Company
P.O. Box 791
Harrisonburg, VA 22801-0791
3 common and 3 sweet

Wilton's Organic Seed
Potatoes
P.O. Box 28
Aspen, CO 81612
2 varieties of common
potatoes

ORGANIC GARDENING SUPPLIES

Age-Old Garden Supply
P.O. Box 1556
Boulder, CO 80306

Bargyla Rateaver
9049 Covina Street
San Diego, CA 92126
Catalogue for long SASE

Bountiful Gardens (Ecology Action)
5798 Ridgewood Road
Willits, CA 95490

Bricker's Organic Farm
842 Sandbar Ferry Road
Augusta, GA 30901

Earlee, Inc.
2002 Highway 62
Jeffersonville, IN 47130-3556

Earthly Goods Farm & Garden Supply
Route 3, Box 761
Mounds, OK 74047

Full Circle Garden Products
P.O. Box 6
Redway, CA 95560
Catalogue $2.00

Gardener's Supply Company
128 Intervale Road
Burlington, VT 05401

Gardens Alive!
5100 Schenley Place
Lawrenceburg, IN 47025

Green Earth Organics
9422 144th Street East
Puyallap, WA 98373

Growing Naturally
P.O. Box 54
149 Pine Lane
Pineville, PA 18946

Harmony Farm Supply
P.O. Box 460
Graton, CA 95444

Holland's Organic Garden
8515 Stearns
Overland Park, KS 66214

Hortopaper Growing Systems
4111 North Motel Drive,
Suite 101
Fresno, CA 93722

The Natural Gardening Company
217 San Anselmo Avenue
San Anselmo, CA 94960

Necessary Trading Company
One Nature's Way
New Castle, VA 24127-0305

Nitron Industries
P.O. Box 1447
Fayetteville, AR 72702

Ohio Earth Food
13737 Duquette Avenue N.E.
Hartville, OH 44632

Organic Control, Inc.
P.O. Box 781147
Los Angeles, CA 90016

Organic Pest Management
P.O. Box 55267
Seattle, WA 98155

Peaceful Valley Farm Supply
P.O. Box 2209
Grass Valley, CA 95945

Ringer Corporation
9959 Valley View Road
Eden Prairie, MN
55344-3585

POTATO COUNCILS, BOARDS, ASSOCIATIONS AND MUSEUMS

The Potato Board
1385 South Colorado
Boulevard, Suite 512
Denver, CO 80222

National Potato Council
9085 East Mineral Circle,
Suite 155
Englewood, CO 80112

Potato Association of
America
8 Holmes Hall
University of Maine
Orono, ME 04469

Idaho Potato Commission
P.O. Box 1068
Boise, ID 83701

Maine Potato Board
744 Main Street, Suite 9
Presque Isle, ME 04769

Michigan Potato Industry
Commission
13109 Schavey Road, Suite 7
De Witt, MI 48820

Red River Valley Potato
Growers Association
P.O. Box 301
East Grand Forks, MN 56721

Oregon Potato Commission
700 N.E. Multnomah, Suite
460
Portland, OR 97232

Washington State Potato
Commission
108 Interlake
Moses Lake, WA 98837

Wisconsin Potato and
Vegetable Growers
Association
700 Fifth Avenue, P.O. Box
327
Antigo, WI 54409

The Potato Museum
P.O. Box 791
Great Falls, VA 22066
(703) 759-6714

Sweet Potato Council of the
United States
P.O. Box 14, Marsh Hill Road
McHenry, MD 21541-0014

Mississippi Sweet Potato
Council
P.O. Box 5207
Mississippi State, MS 39762

Louisiana Sweet Potato
Commission
P.O. Box 113—Yambilee
Building
Opelousas, LA 70571-0113

North Carolina Sweet Potato
Commission
4008-201A Barrett Drive
Raleigh, NC 27609

Bibliography

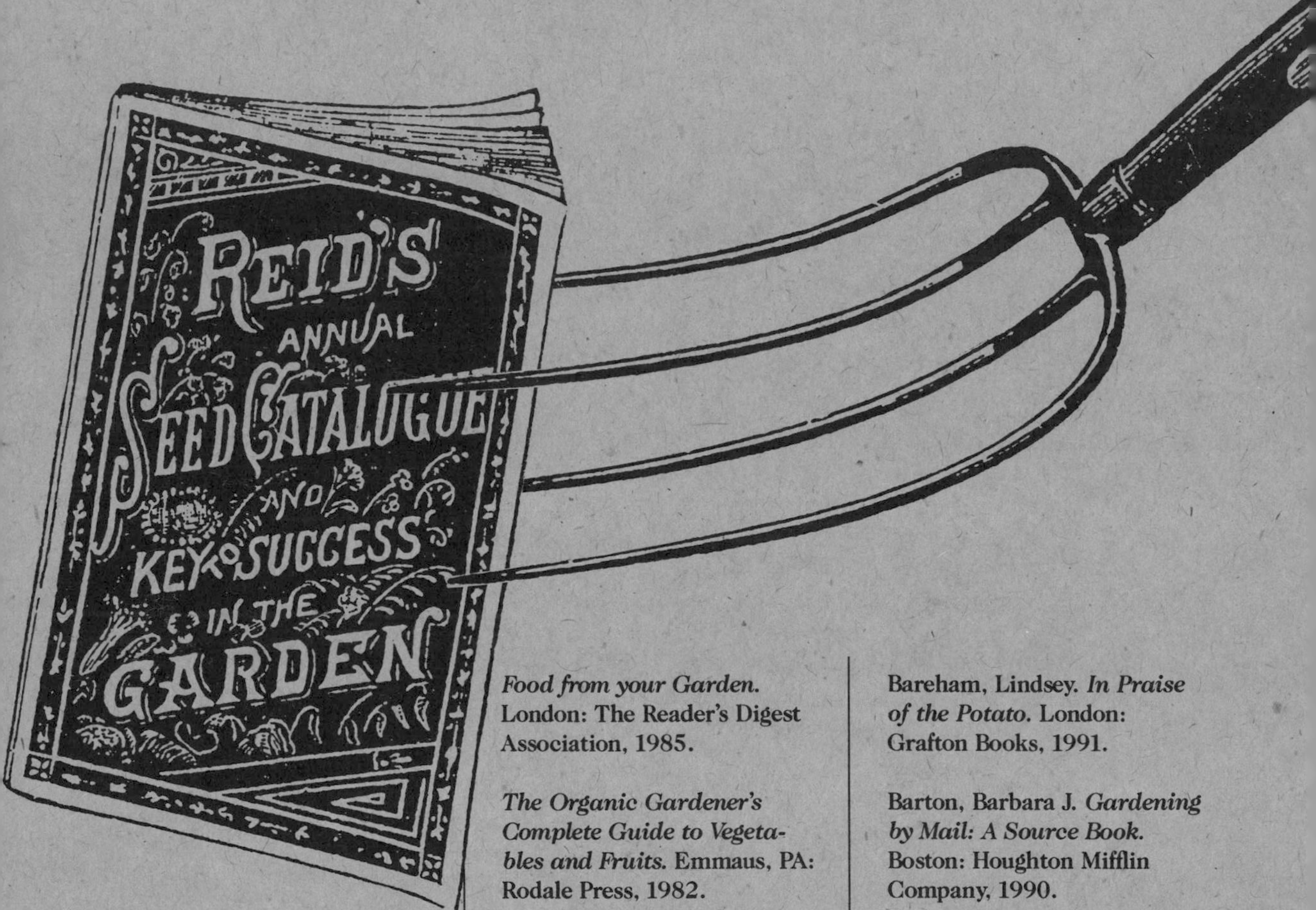

Food from your Garden.
London: The Reader's Digest
Association, 1985.

*The Organic Gardener's
Complete Guide to Vegeta-
bles and Fruits.* Emmaus, PA:
Rodale Press, 1982.

*Gardening: The Complete
Guide to Growing America's
Favorite Fruits & Vegetables.*
Reading, MA: Addison-Wesley
Publishing Company, 1986.

Ball, Jeff. *The Self-Sufficient
Suburban Garden.* Emmaus,
PA: Rodale Press, 1983.

Bareham, Lindsey. *In Praise
of the Potato.* London:
Grafton Books, 1991.

Barton, Barbara J. *Gardening
by Mail: A Source Book.*
Boston: Houghton Mifflin
Company, 1990.

Berolzheimer, Ruth, Editor.
*250 Ways of Serving Po-
tatoes.* Chicago: Consolidated
Book Publishers, 1951.

Coleman, Eliot. *The New
Organic Grower.* Chelsea,
VT: Chelsea Green, 1989.

Cornog, Mary W. *Growing and Cooking Potatoes.* Dublin, NH: Yankee, 1981.

Correll, Donovan S. *The Potato and its Wild Relatives.* Renner, TX: Texas Research Foundation, 1962.

————. *Section Tuberarium of the Genus Solanum of North America and Central America.* Washington, DC: United States Department of Agriculture, 1952.

Creasy, Rosalind. *The Complete Book of Edible Landscaping.* San Francisco: Sierra Club Books, 1982.

————. *Cooking from the Garden.* San Francisco: Sierra Club Books, 1988.

De Saulles, Denys. *Home Grown.* Boston: Houghton Mifflin, 1988.

Doty, Walter. L. *All About Vegetables.* San Ramon, CA: Ortho Books, 1990.

Fell, Derek. *Vegetables: How to Select, Grow and Enjoy.* Tucson, AZ: HP Books, 1982.

Fortey, Jackie, Editor. *The Complete Potato.* London: Hunkydory Designs Limited in conjunction with The Juniper Press, 1981.

Hobhouse, Henry. *Seeds of Change.* New York: Harper & Row, Publishers, 1986.

Hughes, Meredith Sayles and E. Thomas. *The Great Potato Book.* New York: Macmillan Publishing Company, 1986.

Jabs, Carolyn. *The Heirloom Gardener.* San Francisco: Sierra Club Books, 1984.

Jones, Jeanne. *Stuffed Spuds.* New York: M. Evans and Company, 1982.

Leighton, Ann. *Early American Gardens "For Meate or Medicine".* Amherst, MA: The University of Massachusetts Press, 1986.

Minnich, Jerry. *Gardening for Maximum Nutrition.* Emmaus, PA: Rodale Press, 1983.

Mother Earth News Editors. *The Healthy Garden Handbook.* New York: Simon & Schuster, 1989.

Newcomb, Duane and Karen. *The Complete Vegetable Gardener's Sourcebook.* New York: Prentice Hall Press, 1989.

Ogden, Shepherd and Ellen. *The Cook's Garden.* Emmaus, PA: Rodale Press, 1989.

Olkowski, William, Sheila Daar, and Helga Olkowski. *Common-Sense Pest Control.* Newtown, CT: The Taunton Press, 1991.

Rogers, Mara Reid. *The International Spud.* Boston: Little, Brown and Company, 1992.

Rupp, Rebecca. *Blue Corn & Square Tomatoes.* Pownal, VT: Storey Communications, Inc., 1987.

Scott, Maria Luisa and Jack Denton. *The Great Potato Cookbook.* New York: Bantam Books, 1980.

Shepherd, Renee and Fran Raboff. *Recipes From A Kitchen Garden Volume Two.* Felton, CA: Shepherd's Garden Publishing, 1991.

Splittstoesser, W.E. *Vegetable Growing Handbook.* New York: Van Nostrand Reinhold, 1984.

Steffens, Gael McM. *The National Gardening Book of Potatoes.* Burlington, VT: National Gardening Association, 1985.

Tannahall, Reay. *Food In History.* New York: Stein and Day/Publishers, 1973.

Van Patten, George F. *Organic Garden Vegetables.* Portland, OR: Van Patten Publishing, 1991.

White, Susan, editor. *Weisenberger Cookbook II.* Midway, KY: Weisenberger Mills.

Young, D.J. *Potatoes, Sweet and Irish.* Pownal, VT: Storey Communications, 1977.

Index